Ka

HIP GUIDE TORONTO

Macfarlane Walter & Ross
TORONTO

Macfarlane Walter & Ross
37A Hazelton Avenue
Toronto, Canada M5R 2E3

Canadian Cataloguing in Publication Data

von Hahn, Karen, 1961-
Hip guide to Toronto
Includes index.
ISBN 0-921912-99-4

1. Toronto (Ont.) - Guidebooks.   2. Restaurants - Ontario - Toronto - Guidebooks.
I. Title.

FC3097.18.V65 1996   917.13′541044   C96-931286-5
F1059.5.T683V65 1996

Printed and bound in Canada

THE PUBLISHER ACKNOWLEDGES THE SUPPORT OF THE ONTARIO ARTS COUNCIL
AND THE CANADA COUNCIL

To Thomas, Sophie and Philip

Many thanks to Leanne, Beth, Pippa & Chris,
Liba, Jan, Gary & John and my parents, Susan & Perce.

CONTENTS

INTRODUCTION

When I was a kid growing up in the sixties, my parents had a book called *It's Hard To Be Hip Over 30*. Even though I was little and completely clueless on the subject of hip, this slim satirical book fascinated me. Now that I'm grown, with two small kids of my own and definitely past that strict age limit, I beg to differ.

To me, hip has no rules: no age constraints, no style requirements, no strictures of practice or behaviour. And, contrary to the widely held belief of those in the mass media striving to instruct their readers, viewers and listeners in the latest cool thing, you cannot learn to be hip. Studying *Vogue*, "Friends" or MTV for clues on how to wear your hair, dress, talk and appear "hip" is fruitless. Today, drinking espresso and sporting a beat goatee is practically the norm; to be truly hip requires you to wake up, abandon your sheeplike behaviour and develop your own cutting-edge sensibility.

Being hip in Toronto takes a little effort: only recently has last call been extended past 1:00 a.m. and for almost six months of the year you have to dress like Nanook of the North just to survive. But, unlike other truly hip places, it's livable. You can drive around and actually park outside a lot of places; get in to great shows and restaurants with minimal hassle; and live in a cool old house right downtown with neat shops and cafés just around the corner.

Being hip here isn't cliché – performance-art pieces about ritual scarification where the deep and sober patrons are uniformly clad in black. To me, hip is found in the inherent soul of a place or event; it's driving out of your way just to pass by the giant Penaten jar on Bathurst at Dundas, or refusing to even enter a dollar store, yet jumping at any opportunity to visit Honest Ed's. Being hip here is about riding the Queen streetcar with the kids to the end of the line just for the sights along the way, or picking up Penrose's fish & chips wrapped in newspaper and spending the afternoon exploring tombstones in the Mount Pleasant Cemetery. Or Saturday mornings at Kensington Market, whole afternoons at Holt's, last call at the Cameron and grabbing a slice from Pizza Gigi on your way home. Many truly hip places here aren't the latest or the trendiest. Many are actually sort of quaint or downright *un*cool, but what they do have is their very own identity and style.

The thing to remember is, just as right after you stop trying to meet someone you can fall madly in love, once you can stand back and see the charm and humour in the most ordinary of things and places, you may find a new way of looking at hip.

where to eat

TRULY RELAXING

What makes a restaurant truly relaxing is that all the right elements are in place: the food is great, you're not desperately searching through a bizarre menu for some crumb to eat, it isn't creepy to be there, and you can hang out over a juicy dinner, even when you're feeling a tad weak to deal. First on the list of truly relaxing places to chow down is **TRATTORIA GIANCARLO** on College Street. The low-key ambience notwithstanding, this restaurant just exudes good karma. And it serves up great food: a mean grilled veal chop with olives, or a pasta with red sauce and giant juicy grilled shrimp that could be bottled as Memories of Rome. It's small, neither empty nor full, and pretty after its stylish spruce-up, with laquered millwork filling its Victorian-beaded glass storefront and a summer patio out of *West Side Story*. **SOTTO SOTTO** on Avenue Road is crazier, but still delicious and *intime*. A dark and drippy candlelit cavern with a hyperactive open kitchen and in-your-face wait staff, it's slightly silly but still fun. Try the pungent pasta con funghi. You can talk them into customizing huge platters of mixed pasta and grilled stuff to share.

Designers Walk bistro **LE PARADIS** is a restaurant you can always face. It's slightly dingy in true continental style, with reliable steak frites (order extra of the frites part) or saucy variety meats, a good-looking crowd and a cheap yet drinkable red-wine list. Great late on your own or with a big unruly group. The appropriately jaded French-speaking staff maintain their haute Gallic attitude no matter what you throw at them.

CAFE LA GAFFE makes it on this list just because it's so cozy, in a pleasurably dark old Baldwin Street storefront. Almost everyone else you know is there seeking refuge, even though the food is a bit of an issue. You can get by on the chicken dijon entrée, as long as it's accompanied by sufficient glasses of red wine. The central bar is nice, too – smokers can comfortably hop back and forth. Across the street is the poetic JOHN'S ITALIAN CAFFE, with its inspired Palermo/Hoosier interior, honestly aged with tobacco smoke. A hangout, really, with edible pizza, good tunes and best of all, cheap red wine in short shot-style glasses.

Teeny, tiny ARLEQUIN is a must for the nicoise olive fanatic; the entire menu seems dedicated to that humble yet vital fruit. Tight conditions here make for extremely intimate conversations (you can, in fact, usually enjoy your neighbours' with impunity) over very delicious, very Côte d'Azur French food, like aioli, legumes and nightshade vegetables. Similarly puny is TEMPEST. Crammed with tables at which New Agey, perhaps lactose-intolerant, vegan floral arrangers nibble at its weird though tasty menu, the little restaurant still manages to be relaxing despite the din, perhaps because of the pretty sky-like ceiling.

Uptown, FILIPPO shows us how Italian should be done – simply prepared fresh food in an unforced, authentic setting: fantastic crispy pizza with esoteric toppings (though I'd recommend the basic Americano or the ever-elegant margherita), leafy salads of balsamic vinegar and al dente pasta. But what's cool here is that the food comes quickly, and in the summer the waiters are charmingly unorthodox, willing to go across the street to buy popsicles for your kids or get the kitchen to whip up dishes off-menu. More relaxed Italian vibes with a family-run flavour at College Street staple **GIOVANNA**. Cute waiters rush around between the feasting tables, juggling bright ceramic pitchers of house red and jumbo platters of crispy calamari fritti, pizza or simple pasta, and, as at any good family event, you leave having eaten, talked and drunk too much. Same story at the Queen Street West **MASSIMO**, particularly good for a gang, with its long wooden tables *alla rustiche*. One small problem is that the accompanying naif wooden benches become a little tiresome after an extended evening.

Cozy but still glam, downtown **AVALON** offers elegant sanctuary. Around a perplexing central fireplace, groovy business types who like their comforts refined nibble on delicately sauced chicken with their mashed potatoes. Washed down with a fancy red and carefully followed with a perfect little sweet, this is sophisticated soul food. And the service is so observant, you'll feel as if you're in some sort of truly relaxing institute as opposed to a mere restaurant.

And, welcome to the latest new thing: '60s Scandinavian, George Jensen cool, as styled by **BLU** at the corner of Adelaide and Peter Streets. The menu is anything but northern – spiced Carib grills and roti – but the scene is deliciously spare. A pale panel-plywood bar faces a lab-style stainless counter of medicinal-looking liquor bottles.

A small blue Boda Nova bud vase sporting a single yellow daisy finishes the paper-topped, chrome-legged tables. Vodka drinking is required here. Cool jazz and R&B playing on the tables, natch.

TRATTORIA GIANCARLO: 41 Clinton Street T: 533-9619

SOTTO SOTTO: 116A Avenue Road T: 962-0011

LE PARADIS: 166 Bedford Road T: 921-0995

CAFE LA GAFFE: 24 Baldwin Street T: 596-2397

JOHN'S ITALIAN CAFFE: 27 Baldwin Street T: 596-8848

ARLEQUIN: 134 Avenue Road T: 928-9521

TEMPEST: 468 College Street T: 944-2440

FILIPPO'S GOURMET PIZZERIA: 744 St. Clair West T: 658-0568

GIOVANNA: 637 College Street T: 538-2098

MASSIMO PIZZA & PASTA: 504 Queen Street West T: 867-1803

AVALON: 270 Adelaide Street West T: 979-9918

BLU: 340 Adelaide Street West T: 506-9366

ALMOST THERE

Some places have unbelievable food, but miss on the atmosphere. More places are gorgeous to look at but the food is nasty or they're trying way too hard. These spots aren't a total miss, they're just *almost* there.

Groovy **GIO'S** is so cool it has no sign, just a giant schnoz hanging over the door. The tiny open kitchen, vinyl-covered tables and ceiling of hanging clotheslines add to the charm. The kitschy mom-and-pop menu (say, lasagne) is also sort of fun, but as at any Italian tourist trap, the food is not the main attraction. Across the street is **GRANO**, what must surely be the Yonge-and-Eglinton restaurant branch of the Italian Trade Commission, Tuscany Division. Everything Italian is for sale here, from focaccia to Italian conversation classes, all served up on bright, primitif hand-glazed ceramic dishes. Despite the slightly contrived feel, it can be fun to share one of the tasty antipasto platters on a weekday afternoon, about the only time when you can get in without having to line up.

There are many great things about the **ROSEDALE DINER** – the amusing aluminum-fronted building with its tiny bar and funky library wallpaper, for instance; unfortunately, there's not much to eat, especially if the kitchen happens to be out of roast chicken. But people always seem to end up here anyway, especially on a howling night, because you can leave your car parked across the street in the Summerhill LCBO parking lot and simply run across. Yuppie brasserie **ZOLA** suffers an affliction of a different sort. No matter how good your steak frites, you can't help feeling you're in the Paris section of the Epcot Center. It tries valiantly to conceal its Yorkville-mall setting – elaborate Guimard-style Paris Metro transoms conceal the otherwise featureless low ceiling, and Gallic waiters attend to one's every need – but fails to achieve effortlessness. Still, if you can get over that sensation, this is one of the few good places in Yorkville to eat after a movie at the Cumberland Theatre.

There are so many great restaurants on College Street, it's completely understandable to give up on **COCO LEZZONE**, but judging by the regular crowd happily sampling substandard food on uncomfortable seats in this echo chamber, there are few who share my point of view. If you like your pasta with vodka, Pernod or smoked salmon, go ahead and knock yourself out. On the other hand, there's something about **PETER PAN** that I still like, even if it has fallen out of favour. The food's only okay

(the pad Thai is atrocious; the burgers are pretty good), but this big old Victorian diner with its tin ceilings and dark booths is reminiscent of when Queen Street West was truly boho. You half expect Carol Pope to strut in at any moment with Dusty Springfield. Another once-great place currently suffering from a food problem is the RIVOLI, with its sort of Asian/voodoo twist on the Peter Pan diner ambience. The Riv is always an inspiring place to eat late, with its clammy, dimly lit booths of shaved and pierced individuals expressing their alternative sexuality. Unfortunately, the kitchen, which used to be a Laotian marvel, is seriously malfunctioning of late (same menu, new chef).

The seriously over-the-top MILDRED PIERCE, with its so fabulous theatrical interior (gold lamé, sumptuous banquettes) and warehousey King West filmdistrict location, overhandles food that overstays its welcome later in the evening. This tends to tarnish the glimmer. Harbord Street MESSIS does the requisite pizza-and-pasta thing (and within everyone's acceptable price point), so it's always packed. You'll need a reservation if you want to join the upscale crowd searching for something appealing to eat from the overly ambitious, silly menu (big fans of the skyscraper-construction dish here). Same crowd at CITIES (big surprise, same creator), which is weird, because of its very west Queen location (we're talking Mental Health Centre here). But the maître d' is a highly sensitive individual, the food is delicious (as in the mille-feuille scalloped potatoes) and they mean to feed you.

Actually, there's absolutely nothing wrong with **KIT KAT**. It's one of the only places along King Street with any real identity (except for Ed's Warehouse, of course). Always stylish, even back when it was just a little tiny café, and Big Al Carbone himself was manning all fronts. Now it's packed, the people are chichi CPI–types and it's a real restaurant. Yummy grilled Italian sausage and frites and lightly handled pasta are served up mass picnic–style, with the energy level cranked up high. You would be hard-pressed to find this spot relaxing, but it's particularly convenient before a game at the Dome, unless you're the type who would rather dine on-site on $6 microwaved nachos-and-chips in a paper container.

GIO'S: 2070 Yonge Street T: 932-2306

GRANO: 2035 Yonge Street T: 440-1986

ROSEDALE DINER: 1164 Yonge Street T: 923-3122

ZOLA: 162 Cumberland Street T: 515-1222

COCO LEZZONE: 602 College Street T: 535-1489

PETER PAN: 375 Queen Street West T: 593-0917

MILDRED PIERCE: 99 Sudbury Street T: 588-5695

MESSIS: 97 Harbord Street T: 920-2186

CITIES: 859 Queen Street West T: 504-3762

KIT KAT BAR & GRILL: 297 King Street West T: 977-4461

GLAM NIGHT

Sometimes the tried-and-true regulars just won't do. Say it's your birthday, or you're trying to convince friends from out of town that Toronto is a city worth living in, or maybe you feel like putting on a lot of makeup and interacting with glittering strangers. The ultimo spot for such glamorous yearnings is Susur Lee's tasty downtown jewel, **LOTUS**. The crowd is monied, with a sophisticated palate and patience. Little, highly expensive works of edible art like those offered at Lotus are best enjoyed on an expense account. Unfortunately, the rigour of the kitchen spills over into the dining room and creates an inhibiting hush. But very yummy things on the menu. Eat lots; it's so expensive that you'll feel guilty coming back soon.

Driving into **SCARAMOUCHE** in the classic Benvenuto building, you feel as fabulous as Jane Hathaway pulling up to her apartment in her open Cadillac convertible. Valet parking completes the picture, and once inside, your Beverley Hills fantasy continues with a sparkling night view of the city (great for out-of-towners), and an urbane, casual crowd trading witticisms over the gentle clinking of glasses. Unquestionably, the fancy dining room is actually less glam, populated mainly by docile pensioners searching in vain for something to eat with fewer than seventeen ingredients. The cool kids want to sit in the pasta bar. Not only is the food better (simpler pastas and grills) than in the dining room, but you get to lounge in the '70s-modern conversation pit. Nice long bar, well stocked with olives and house chippies; also a vantage point for sussing out the crowd. Very good snackies: the wildly woody mushroom pasta in a black truffle broth; the roast chicken and risotto; and the amazing pies, especially the coconut cream. Some words of advice: don't overdue it on the complimentary garlic bean purée unless you have a deep-seated fear of vampires.

LA FENICE is another glam restaurant that's charmingly lost in the me decade, somewhere near Milan. Its sober, sterile interior and grown-up crowd tend to keep the hip kids away, but sometimes this can be a blessing. And the food is truly extraordinary: deftly prepared delicate northern pasta like agnolotti or crespelle, piquant antipasto dashingly served in a trolley, and beautiful veal or seafood. Hushed and private, and important to remember as a key refuge for the working or theatregoing set. There is also a cheaper bistretto downstairs, but it's typically underpopulated (probably because of the excruciatingly uncomfortable triangular bar chairs).

There's an aura of glamour at the brand-new **XANGO** that takes you on a quick trip to old Havana, first-class. It's not really in the decor (a sort of Mission revival of the former Orso on John Street) but in the fabulous Latin beat of the truly inspired menu. Start with one of the four ceviches (oysters are best) washed down with a crisp martini. You'll bliss out over the camarones with black beans and rice, maybe a little rapini with burnt garlic on the side. When you've had your fill, sit back, groove to the salsa and play Castro with a fat and stinky Cuban cigar.

Soulful **CHIADO** is old-world cool. A fancy Portuguese restaurant on College Street with manly waiters, a full wine list with surprises from the Duoro region, and the attentions of charming, handsome chef-owner Albino Silva, this is a truly a glam place to linger over a great meal. Love the fresh white cheese drizzled with olive oil appetizer thing, too. **JOSO'S** on Davenport Road is another hetero sort of restaurant with a unique atmosphere. The macho 'tude is expressed in the strange breast obsession of Joso, its Dalmatian sculptor-owner. He has festooned every nook and cranny with pendulous mammary pairs of various finishes and materials that have the combined effect of multiple sets of staring eyeballs. Trickier still, you get a nice close look at your glassy-eyed sea specimen (the wait staff will bring it to your table and actually stroke it) before it is delicately grilled to your satisfaction. Besides the amazing, slightly smoky grilled fish, try the sexy spaghetti with black squid ink.

Less soul, more glitter at midtown **BISTRO 990**. Great celeb-spotting amid faux Matissesketched wine-cellar walls. Terrific for a glass of champagne and some really French treat, say, a crusty gratin or salade tiede. The shiny **MERCER STREET GRILL** is snazzy like an Upper East Side New York neighbourhood restaurant. There is a pleasant buzz about the groovy narrow space, and the crispy-skinned salmon with wehani rice and baby bok choy is out of this world. Too bad about the dumb zigzags on the wall; the space would have been pretty if it had been done straight.

LOTUS: 96 Tecumseth Street T: 504-7620

SCARAMOUCHE: 1 Benvenuto Place T: 961-8011

LA FENICE: 319 King Street West T: 585-2377

XANGO: 106 John Street T: 593-4407

CHIADO: 864 College Street T: 538-1910

JOSO'S: 202 Davenport Road T: 925-1903

BISTRO 990: 990 Bay Street T: 921-9990

MERCER STREET GRILL: 36 Mercer Street T: 599-3399

SEE AND BE SEEN

Where you sit at **PREGO DELLA PIAZZA** is key. The maître d' must go through hell trying to keep straight the "regular" tables of all kinds of operatives. Politicos, the ladies-who-lunch and entertainment types all make this restaurant their turf, especially in summer in the outdoor courtyard surrounding the Church of the Redeemer. The less rich but more beautiful are generally found next door at **ENOTECA**. Same Cal/Ital menu, brighter lights. At **MARKETTA**, Livent bigwigs and money guys are usually the ones struggling to be heard in the din over a mixed plate of the just-passable antipasti. But food's not the point – what you come here for is the energizing buzz.

NORTH 44 on Yonge Street is pretty in a spare, green-glass uptown way. Lawyers and businesspeople on expense accounts are the only ones who can afford to regularly sample the Asian/Italian-influenced vertical food sculpted by celeb chef Mark McEwan, so you can't exactly call this place fun. Bustling **CENTRO**, across the street, is more fun, with its mixed crowd of the empowered class and the monied Woodbridge dressy Italian crowd, schmoozing over chef Marc Thuet's little delicacies of French origin and a highly palatable wine list. A weird combination, especially in the Northern Italian rustic interior, but the bustle and glitz make this a great place for a celebratory event. Good divorcée wine bar downstairs.

Another power-broker destination is **SPLENDIDO**, the Harbord Street outpost of glam, in a neighbourhood typically associated with glutinous student fare. Popular with the arts and entertainment crowd, this seriously overrated restaurant is well designed for viewing others viewing you. The superfluous valet parking and extremely attentive bartender are also draws, but do not completely overcome the atmosphere which recalls a fancier Pat and Mario's.

Downtown, **JUMP** is a largely Johnny-option crowd, all checking out the deals going down at neighbouring tables in the airy courtyard. All the better to see just who is with whom. Same deal at the other Peter Oliver production, the new TD Tower treehouse **CANOE**. All the right ingredients – once again, executive chef Michael Bonacini, Yabu Pushelberg interior and a lake view – make this a safe bet for power brokering. Better titles here, you can see it in their suits.

What will happen with chef-artiste Greg Couillard's latest self-titled venture, **COUILLARD'S**, remains to be seen. Gastronomes who like tiny cutout cow carrots on the edge of their plates will no doubt flock to be observed at this new Queen Street eatery. And the food – well, remember, this is the guy who brought us jump-up soup in the '80s. Who knows what gastronomic inventions yet await us, and, with his track record, how long Couillard's will stay open.

PREGO DELLA PIAZZA: 150 Bloor Street West **T:** 920-9900

MARKETTA: 138 Avenue Road **T:** 924-4447

NORTH 44: 2537 Yonge Street **T:** 487-4897

CENTRO: 2472 Yonge Street **T:** 483-2211

SPLENDIDO: 88 Harbord Street **T:** 929-7788

JUMP: Commerce Court East, Wellington Street West **T:** 363-3400

CANOE: TD Tower, 66 Wellington Street West **T:** 364-0054

COUILLARD'S: 325 Queen Street West **T:** 597-8608

GROUP ACTIVITIES

When you're with a large group, you want to go to the kind of place that encourages a party atmosphere, a comfortable, cheap place that accommodates you physically, with larger or longer tables, and spiritually gets you rocking.

Best bets for this kind of evening are places with a weird and funky atmosphere, maybe even a live show. My favourite performance restaurants are the **SULTAN'S TENT** and **DON QUIJOTE**. The **SULTAN'S TENT**, though unfortunately located in a bleak Bay Street mini-mall, transports you to a Moroccan bazaar once you're inside. You sit cross-legged on carpeted pillows around a giant brass serving piece sharing yummy little scented purses of food and are entertained by a curiously compelling belly dancer who jiggles over your dinner. Less of a sensory delight, but more visibly loin-stirring is the histrionic art of flamenco. Even though College Street's **DON QUIJOTE** has been there for years, nobody seems to know it's there. Downstairs, you can dine all by yourself at long tables on some pedestrian paella then trek upstairs with a few other lost souls for the truly dynamite flamenco.

Another good group-bonding thing is food you have to share to enjoy. The latest greatest hangout for the Hong Kong investor class is **LAI WAH HEEN** in the newly renovated Metropolitan Hotel on Chestnut Street, the site of the city's original Chinatown. Here you'll find fancy Cantonese and dim sum at flamboyant Hong Kong prices. One of the best Chinese banquets south of Highway 7 is the **GRAND YATT DYNASTY** in the Westin Harbour Castle. It's hard to believe, but you can have a lot of fun in this brightly lit, rather frightening (coral and teal) hotel dining hall. Try the juicy dim sum but avoid the dish that resembles fish sticks with creamed corn or the sweet almond soup, also known as wet kleenex in a bowl. All of the dishes here, however, have symbolic meaning: if you inquire, you can work out a dinner that will promote longevity or happiness.

For dim sum feasting, modest Baldwin Street **KOWLOON** offers the city's best, along with succulent double lobster platters all the better for group groping. **WAH SING**, down the street, excels at lobster with ginger and green onion, and boasts big round tables with lazy Susans to keep the dishes moving. But forget showing up in a large group on Sunday nights, this place is too popular for that kind of cavalier attitude.

The best Ethiopian restaurant in the city, **QUEEN OF SHEBA**, is great for large groups because of the nature of Ethiopian cuisine, which encourages togetherness. Wet and hot lentil or meat stews (*injera*) are meant to be scooped up with absorbent waffle-like pieces of wot (a cross between roti and a J-cloth), plus more belly-dancing potential. Authentic Mexican hangout **MARGARITAS**, on Baldwin

Street, serves up fat, limey versions of the drink, as well as good share-y stuff: salsa, guac and tortilla chips in Aztec-looking stone bowls.

Greek/Med places suit a mob, too, with their extensive tidbit selection (hummus, taramosalata). The show at CHRISTINA'S (belly dancing) and the eighteen-plus appetizer thingies make it an ideal rest stop for a gang out for a night of revelry. However, the Danforth restaurant du jour is definitely the less traditional PAN. Despite its ill-conceived interior (what's with the plaster cherubs and high-tech lighting plan?), it has good group potential with lots of room for a big table and delish funky Greek-with-a-twist food: lima beans with feta and artichoke/potato surprise. Even so, I prefer the low-key atmosphere and simple traditional Greek fare at the neighbouring OMONIA – especially in the summer, when you can hang endlessly at their tiny corner patio snacking and drinking. More noshing on bits and bites at College Street pool hall MIDTOWN, which has surprisingly delicious and cheap tapas from lunch through evening. Uptown, JERUSALEM is hardly *au courant* (it's been there for decades and shows every bit of its age), but the tasty Middle Eastern standards like falafel and baba ghanouj are great for ordering en masse and sharing with friends. Grim but good.

SULTAN'S TENT: 1280 Bay Street T: 961-0601

DON QUIJOTE: 300 College Street T: 922-7636

LAI WAH HEEN: Metropolitan Hotel, 118 Chestnut Street T: 977-9899

GRAND YATT DYNASTY: Westin Harbour Castle, 1 Harbor Square T: 869-3663

KOWLOON: 5 Baldwin Street T: 977-3773

WAH SING: 47 Baldwin Street T: 599-8822

QUEEN OF SHEBA: 1198 Bloor Street West T: 536-4162

MARGARITAS: 14 Baldwin Street T: 977-5525

CHRISTINA'S: 535 Danforth Avenue T: 463-4418

OMONIA RESTAURANT & TAVERN: 426 Danforth Avenue T: 465-2129

PAN ON THE DANFORTH: 516 Danforth Avenue T: 466-8158

MIDTOWN: 552 College Street T: 920-4533

JERUSALEM: 955 Eglinton Avenue West T: 783-6494

PLACES TO REALLY EAT

When you're starved for soul-satisfying food, perhaps after a few too many mediocre eating experiences (or after a few too many cocktails the night before), there are some tried-and-true places where you know you can really chow down. Everyone claims to have found the city's best Chinese food restaurant, but to my mind you can always find it at **LEE GARDEN** on Spadina Avenue. You may have to wait in what seems like an endless line, especially on Sundays, or be seated at a large table with a group of people you've never laid eyes on, but at least you can swoon over their fabulous hot and sour soup, ginger lobster, chicken with asparagus in black bean sauce, sizzling pork loin and sautéed snowpea greens. If it's Lao/Thai food you're after (that citrus and heat craving), **VANIPHA LANNA** on Eglinton West is your best bet. The aromatic lemongrass shrimp soup, non-ketchupy pad Thai and yummy sticky rice are deliciously comforting, especially when consumed at one of their tiny Ikat-padded boothlets. The restaurant's downtown downstairs relative **VANIPHA** in Kensington Market isn't half-bad either.

For dumplings, it's definitely old-tyme **PETER'S CHUNG KING**, at the somewhat forlorn corner of College and Spadina. They're perfectly fried, meaty and juicy, eminently edible. Fuelled by large pots of tea, it's surprising how many of those little doggies you can put down. For pizza, should you have the patience to truck all the way up Dufferin Street, wait for a table and finally get served, the most extraordinary 'za is to be found at **CAMARRA**. The focaccia-like crust, crispy with parmesan, is especially good topped with black olives and washed down with a nasty Brio.

If you feel like pigging out on Indian (legumes and layered spicing), the most sophisticated place in town is the scary **CUISINE OF INDIA**, way the hell out in Mel's territory on Yonge at Sheppard in a tiny self-plaza, landscaped with parking out front and nasty brown shag carpeting inside. It's only a destination for the exceptional tandoori and happily offbeat interpretations of classic Indian cuisine. Nirvana can be reached more conveniently at **NATARAJ** on Bloor West, a grey laminate room with a mirrored bar as its centrepiece. Curiously, the wait staff is Chinese, adding a certain *je ne sais quoi* to the otherwise featureless atmosphere. They bring out exceptional onion bhaji and dal, and a gorgeous tandoori cauliflower left whole and charred orange, to a mostly U of T prof-and-student crowd.

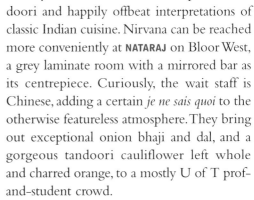

When only raw fish will do, you can go crazy at beautiful indigo blue-walled **NAMI**, accompanied by teapotsful of hot sake or big Kirin drafts. Unless you are a fussy sushi eater, the giant Love Boats are a riot, as are the giggling kimono-clad waitresses who are never astounded by how much you snack. Sit at either bar (sushi or robata), or for conversation, in one of the womblike tatami rooms. But if it's flesh you're after – either a bloody steak or the meat of a steamed lobster to douse in drawn butter – head for the kitschy **HOUSE OF CHAN**. Tanks of live crustaceans and slabs of the finest U.S. prime await. You can sit in one of the dim red vinyl banquettes and eat bowls of cottage-fried potatoes and onions just like at the Palm in New York. I guarantee, some guy you barely know who's in real estate will come over to shake your hand and say you look terrific.

LEE GARDEN: 331 Spadina Avenue T: 593-9524

VANIPHA LANNA: 471 Eglinton Avenue West T: 484-0895

VANIPHA FINE CUISINE: 193 Augusta Avenue T: 340-0491

CUISINE OF INDIA: 5222 Yonge Street T: 229-0377

NATARAJ: 394 Bloor Street West T: 928-2925

PETER'S CHUNGKING: 281 College Street T: 928-2936

CAMARRA PIZZERIA: 2899 Dufferin Street T: 789-3221

NAMI: 55 Adelaide Street East T: 362-7373

HOUSE OF CHAN: 876 Eglinton Avenue West T: 781-5575

GIRLIE FOOD

There are times when you have to inhale masses of food and others when a light little something will do. Guys, unless attempting to impress, will complain bitterly if they are forced to subsist on a canapé; not so with girls. Here are a few suggestions to please the girlie palate.

Queen of girlie cuisine is **KALENDAR KOFFEE HOUSE**. Despite the gag-me spelling, really this is a very pretty café and wine bar. They will feed you, too, with yummy scroll things that are a sort of '90s version of a crepe. The roll-up of choice is the Number 6 with chicken, avocado and plum tomatoes, all folded in a log that sits alone on the middle of your plate – infuriatingly inadequate for any member of the male persuasion.

More manly perhaps are the bivalves offered in abundance at **RODNEY'S OYSTER HOUSE**. Choose the smallest ones and douse with vodka and fresh horseradish or one of their campy sauces (try the Poor White Trash hot sauce). Remember, don't chew, just suck and swallow. Also chewy are the robust Italian sandwiches and pizza that accompany your drink at **FRITZ**, a lacquered jewel box in Yorkville Mews. If you're feeling peckish, sample one of their perfectly layered rustic sandwiches on crusty peasant bread along with a Spumanti at happy hour, Florentine-style.

And nobody can convince me that people actually go to **SOTTOVOCE** for a real dinner. While they do serve up arugula-ish sandwiches or a cute little pasta of the day, those are generally consumed by people too lazy to walk a couple of blocks to **CALIFORNIA SANDWICHES**. Same story at **BAR ITALIA**. Even though the salads and sandwiches are great (in particular, the bresaola and avocado salad and the terracina sandwich), face it – they're sandwiches and salads, not dinner, unless you're in the mood for girlie food.

KALENDAR KOFFEE HOUSE: 546 College Street T: 923-4138

RODNEY'S OYSTER HOUSE: 209 Adelaide Street East T: 363-8105

FRITZ: Old York Lanes, 138 Cumberland Street T: 966-0111

SOTTOVOCE WINE & PASTA BAR: 595 College Street T: 536-4564

CALIFORNIA SANDWICHES: 244 Claremont Street T: 603-3317

BAR ITALIA: 584 College Street T: 535-3621

STARCH AND GREASE

For me, starch and grease is that seriously tired concept "comfort food." Nothing is so essential on a miserable wet afternoon as the slightly sweaty warmth of a good deli. So, keeping in mind that one man's bagel is another man's kimchee, here are the key comfort destinations.

On a grey Sunday evening in November, just as you are recovering from stomach flu and have finished paying all your bills, there's only one place you can go out to dinner: the blissfully East Bloc **KORONA RESTAURANT** on Bloor Street West in the Annex. Here, you can cozy up in a warm booth, and be "soothed" by a selection of truly wacky hits, from the "Green Berets" to the Polish national anthem to Elvis crooning "My Way" – live and Memorex. In this setting, nothing tastes so delicious as a carrot-filled bowl of beef noodle soup and a stately portion of the crunchy wiener schnitzel (so big it hangs off the edge of the plate) with home fries and peppery coleslaw. And although you may be tempted to wash down this fine repast with a Corona beer, remind yourself that the appropriate drink is not a Mexican brew but good old Pilsner Urquell. If you need a little comic relief, you can always order the astoundingly hefty Transylvanian wooden platter for two (two what, you may well ask once it arrives), and you're sure to find more perverse comfort in the brisk waitresses in lace-up boots and the old guys playing chess and smoking in the back. If more of a dairy experience is what you're after, you will have to head up to Lawrence Plaza, unfortunately, because that's where the old leftist **UNITED BAKERS DAIRY RESTAURANT** now lives. Home of blue-ribbon cheese blintzes, varenikes and other ulcer-friendly foods. Though it's not even half the place it was when it was located on Spadina, this restaurant offers treats that can still be relied upon in times of need.

For comfort of a meatier variety, there are, sadly, only a couple of options left. Besides **PANCER'S**, which is way too far north for anyone to contemplate visiting on a regular basis (despite the juicy hand-cut pastrami), there is very little in the way of real delicatessen in the city. Corny as **YITZ'S** may be, it does still serve up a mean corned beef sandwich, which, when eaten with a plate of old dills and a truly freezing draft beer, heals your soul. Unfortunately, you can't stray far from the smoked meat here. One glimpse at a beef knish makes you yearn for the days of the downtown delis like Switzer's. The last downtown smoked meat outpost is the strangely located **CORNED BEEF HOUSE** in the garment district on Adelaide. Juicy not fatty, and delectably salty, this corned beef puts the Druxy's version to shame. If it's wurst you're after, try the crunchy veal sausage with rösti potatoes and fried onions at the Yorkville **MÖVENPICK**. Not a particularly comforting atmosphere with the mass of oversize menus and lined-up U.S. tourists, but a damn fine wurst all the same.

A radical departure from delicatessen but still a comfort food is the humble grilled cheese. The location of the very best grilled cheese sandwich in the city is a well-hidden secret – until now. Out in High Park on Annette Street, across from Annette Public School, **SUNNY BAR**, a cute old variety store with funny '40s windows full of those plants you see in dry cleaners. Inside, there's an old lunch counter where Pete has been making grilled cheese on white for the last thirty years. He sticks them under an old toaster thing and actually butters the outsides, wrapping one end in a napkin for easy eating!

Also comfy is the quintessential fish & chips parlour, **PENROSE FISH & CHIPS** on Mount Pleasant. With wall-mounted trophy fish and photos of old Toronto above the small aqua booths in the rear, a cheery grey-haired waitress bringing you Vernors or malt vinegar and newspaper wrap on takeout, they've got the Brit soul-food thing down just right. That and the crisply fried halibut and chips are why they're still lined up outside on weekends.

For starchy stuff, check out caterer Dinah Koo's latest venture, **TIGER LILY NOODLE HOUSE** on Queen Street West. Here, the modest Asian noodle is prepared in a variety of fashions (cold, stir-fried, in broth) and you pick your noodles and fixings at a counter in the front, like the classic Chinese takeouts of old Toronto. The best of these takeouts still remaining, **INTERNATIONAL CHOP SUEY** on Kingston Road, is worth a visit when Beaching it. Nothing is quite so soul-replenishing as the smell of a piping-hot carton of chow mein to go.

KORONA RESTAURANT: 493 Bloor Street West T: 961-1824

UNITED BAKERS DAIRY RESTAURANT: Lawrence Plaza T: 789-0519

RED PANCER'S DELI: 6233 Bathurst Street T: 223-7870

YITZ'S DELI: 346 Eglinton Avenue West T: 487-4506

CORNED BEEF HOUSE: 303 Adelaide Street West T: 977-2333

MÖVENPICK RESTAURANT: 133 Yorkville Avenue T: 926-9545

SUNNY BAR: 259 Annette Street T: unlisted

PENROSE FISH & CHIPS: 600 Mount Pleasant Road T: 483-6800

TIGER LILY'S: 257 Queen Street West T: 977-5499

INTERNATIONAL CHOP SUEY HOUSE: 955 Kingston Road T: 698-1661

KITSCH VALUE

Some spots are reverse-hip by virtue of kitsch value alone. These are places with fun built right in – all you have to do is show up. Vegetarian restaurant **ANNAPURNA** is a shining example of the truly weird. In the window there are pictures of guru Sri Chinmoy lifting

350 pounds with a single hand. A mixed crowd – undernourished health fanatics and radical lesbians wearing their Calvin Jockeys outside their clothes – sits at plastic tablecloths being served distilled Bathurst and Dupont rain water by sari-clothed Waspy converts. You can't get much farther-out than that. Actually, some of the Indian food is quite delicious, but no booze or smokes obviously. For a totally unhealthy experience, consider visiting the old **DAIRY QUEEN** on Pottery Road. You can drive in and park in back, just like when you were a kid. Arrive in a pickup truck for ultimate chic. The parking lot is situated attractively over the Don Valley and you can enjoy the lovely view while slurping on your blueberry shake in the back of the pickup. A great first date.

On a cold winter evening, try **ED'S WAREHOUSE**, the hysterically packed vaudeville dance hall. Each of Ed's finds makes you want to ask, "Who would make that?" and, better still, "Who would buy it?" Imagine masses of red tables wedged in amongst stuffed birds, oriental urns and signed theatre programs from has-been West End stars like Rula Lenska: "For Ed and Anne with love." Amid this objet overdose (the epic flamboyance is worthy of a Cecil B. deMille set), confused patrons – a mix of pretheatre bus-ins and hacked-up newspaper types, possibly in borrowed jacket and tie – pour down several solid drinkies with their surprisingly delicious roast beef. Order the English cut with the teeny tinned peas and it will arrive terrrifyingly fast. Watch out for the live parrot on the way out. Blissfully dark **TOM JONES STEAKHOUSE** is a bit more of a hushed carnivorous experience. Here, you can drink Chivas instead of rye, eat jumbo shrimp cocktail or stinky caesar salad before diving into your perfectly cooked slab of beef, all in the atmosphere of a private men's club. The funny lost little building even has the ultimate steak-house window of brown and green stained-glass circles that makes even broad daylight dark and mysterious. More ultimate steakhouse atmosphere at the goofy **KEG MANSION**, spiritual home of the high school prom. The only Keg you should go to, it's a classic because of its historic location, the grand old Massey manse. Perfect backdrop for the '70s-style steaks with sautéed mushrooms, toasty sourdough bread and the deadly Keg-size drinks.

Fully functional hipster families will groove to the funny scene at **THE STEAK PIT**, North Toronto's '60s throwback Sunday-night place for steak and ribs. Have your fill of juicy chilled dills and celery while you survey the action from one of the big round tables. A stone's throw away is the dusty old **LOBSTER TRAP**. If cracking and slurping and dipping a perfectly steamed bottom feeder while mopping your butter-slicked chin with an oversize plastic lobster bib is your idea of a good time, this one's for you.

More great lobster and steak at the hilarious yet still packed and popular **HOUSE OF CHAN** on Eglinton Avenue West. This is Chan as in Charlie, complete with Grauman's Chinese Theatre decor. You half expect a gong to sound every time the staff emerge from the kitchen. Try the amazing salmon in black bean sauce or curiously dry Bernie's Salted Ribs. Added Chinese kitsch across the street at **CHINA HOUSE**, one of those places kids love, with a picturesque mini-bridge from which you can throw pennies at goldfish in the bubbling little pond. You sit at large round tables with napkins

folded to look like crowns and feast on the top 40 of Canadian-Chinese: moo goo gai pan, egg rolls and barbecue spare ribs.

Go for the T-bone dinner at cute old Yonge Street **LINDY'S**. Followed by a rice pudding, and washed down with the kind of cocktail you'd see pictured on a paper place mat (a Harvey Wallbanger or a Pink Lady), you may actually enjoy your repast. There's something truly great about this place, which embodies all that is Yonge and Dundas to its clientele of hockey fans, Newfie tourists, hookers and Ryerson students. If old-world romance kitsch is more what you're after, try **L'EUROPE** on Bloor Street West, where you will receive the attentions of the resident gypsy violinist, who, with virtually nobody else to play to, will regale you with Transylvanian classics over your drippy steaks Esterhazy.

At **CICCONE'S**, on King Street near the puzzling Executive Motor Inn, you'll be entertained by the begowned proprietress-in-a-time-warp revelling in her brief brushes with fame. Also drippy chianti-bottle candles and corny red-and-white-checked tablecloths straight out of *Goodfellas*. Good thing, because the food is, well, authentic cheesy Jersey '50s Italian.

For fun of a dinner-dancing variety, **THE OLD MILL**, the legendary Toronto fantasy farm, is just the ticket. Wedding central, with its scenic photo-backdrop mill and dark, timbered-ceiling dining rooms, it serves up not a bad little dinner (try the lamb), especially when interrupted by dips and spins to "Pennies in a Stream." And the presentation of the baked Alaska is just too funny: think many costumed waiters promenading with lit torches.

But truly the funniest restaurant in town might also be one of the best and most expensive. Peter Oliver's little French "chateau," **AUBERGE DU POMMIER** has all the authenticity of a Disney movie set. Its surreal setting (between glassy corporate headquarters on Yonge just below Highway 401), in combination with its super-serious French menu, is enough to keep you laughing, even after the bill arrives.

ANNAPURNA: 1085 Bathurst Street T: 537-8513

DAIRY QUEEN: 1040 Broadview Avenue T: 425-2261

ED'S WAREHOUSE: 270 King Street West T: 593-6676

TOM JONES STEAKHOUSE: 17 Leader Lane T: 366-6583

THE KEG MANSION: 515 Jarvis Street T: 964-6609

THE STEAK PIT: 1666 Avenue Road T: 783-3077

LOBSTER TRAP: 1962 Avenue Road T: 787-3211

HOUSE OF CHAN: 876 Eglinton Avenue West T: 781-5575

CHINA HOUSE: 925 Eglinton Avenue West T: 781-9121

LINDY'S RESTAURANT & TAVERN: 403 Yonge Street T: 977-2131

L'EUROPE: 469 Bloor Street West T: 921-6269

CICCONE'S: 601 King Street West T: 504-5037

THE OLD MILL: 21 Old Mill Road T: 236-2641

AUBERGE DU POMMIER: 4150 Yonge Street T: 222-2220

EGGS ANY STYLE

In the breakfast department, and that means "eggs any style" all day, the downtown **MARS** still rules. Legendary bran muffins and corned beef hash (only on weekends) are the key must-haves. The beehived waitresses are funny and kind, always prepared to bring you more of the dishwater coffee. The frontline action is around the bar at the grill, but remember, if you sit there, you won't get that greasy-spoon smell out of your clothes for days. When the lineups are too intense, say, weekends, consider the often-overlooked **KOS** next door – hardly legendary but a damn fine breakfast.

One of the best plates of eggs (with baked beans and chalah toast, even) can be found at the lovely old **SENATOR** on Victoria Street, across from the back door of the Pantages Theatre. Two drawbacks: it's small, so you'll often have to wait for a table on weekends, and (for breakfast) it's expensive. Waiters with attitude are sorely trying before noon.

The old **FRAN'S** at St. Clair and Yonge (really, the only one that hasn't been ruined through renovation) is still good a.m. fun. All the griddle favourites – pancakes, waffles and deliciously greasy little sausages. One significant drawback, however, is the fake-syrup problem (just what is "table syrup?"). Perhaps fellow sticklers could bring their own maple. Somehow, I always end up at the **AVENUE COFFEE SHOP**, which everybody knows as the Ave./Dav., just like the intersection. It's small and cozy, they take "over-easy" seriously and you can park outside at a Davenport meter. The people are nice here, too – I once saw the grill guy make lunch for a street person. Around the corner is the **MAJESTIC**, which is fun for its Times Square breakfast-spot feeling. The interior is kind of wacky (drippy stucco and dusty-rose panels), but the cook makes a mean feta omelette. Don't forget about **SENIOR'S** at the St. Clair subway, Pleasant Street exit. For toasted westerns and sympathy. Or the **VILLAGE RESTAURANT** in Forest Hill Village, filled with uniformed B.S.S. girls, barelegged in the dead of winter, warming up over fries and gravy, next to real estate agents tucking into banquetburgers and diner coffee.

The arty theatre crowd takes their eggs at **ANGELO'S** in the Annex. It's a retro sort of grill that grew organically over time to accommodate its truly mixed crowd of Hydro workers and CBC types on a break drinking beer. There's a great hungover feeling at the **TASTY RESTAURANT** on Bloor Street West across from Clinton's. A humble Greek diner with little to recommend it besides location, the Tasty does, however, live up to its name. Go for the roast chicken and Greek specialties, as well as the egg thing. An all-day sort of place.

For sheer looks, nothing can beat the poetic **CANARY** on Cherry Street. In its own ramshackle building at the foot of the Leslie Street Spit, it looks as though it's been a diner since Confederation. Kind of scary inside, with pale watery eggs, an intense beery odour and signed photos of second-string celebrities. Slightly less grand but more palatable is the charmingly titled **PATRICIAN GRILL** on King Street East. This place stuck it out on King before the street was happening, and now is reaping the rewards. This is where George Brown College student chefs and furniture retailers go for breakfast.

ALLEN'S on the Danforth does peameal bacon and padas with their eggs. It's mighty easy to blow off a Saturday afternoon here, listening to R&B on the well-stocked jukebox, especially if you follow breakfast with a tangy Bloody Mary.

At pretty **VIENNA HOME BAKERY** on Queen West, you can experience Gay Couillard's incredible eggs with sausage of a dry and spicy variety, all sprinkled with a mysterious herbal substance, in the truly adorable '40s kitchen interior. You can bring home one of Gay's suggestively shaped whole-wheat breads, too.

But after a serious evening out, your best bet is wild **MIMI'S**, conveniently situated beside the old Oak Leaf Steam Baths on Bathurst Street, is the perfect place to stub out cigs in your eggs, feeling wretched and morning-after. Trashy rock and roll, and actually good food if you're not feeling too weak to swallow.

MARS: 432 College Street T: 921-6332

KOS BAR & GRILL: 434 College Street T: 923-1868

SENATOR: 249 Victoria Street T: 364-7517

FRAN'S: 21 St. Clair Avenue West T: 925-6336

AVENUE COFFEE SHOP: 222 Davenport Road T: 924-5191

MAJESTIC RESTAURANT: 150 Avenue Road T: 921-9198

SENIOR'S DINING NOOK: 1397 Yonge Street T: 924-8366

VILLAGE RESTAURANT: 420 Spadina Road T: 487-1420

ANGELO'S RESTAURANT: 268 Howland Avenue T: 533-2297

TASTY RESTAURANT: 692 Bloor Street West T: 537-7553

CANARY GRILL: 409 Front Street East T: 364-9943

PATRICIAN GRILL: 219 King Street East T: 366-4841

ALLEN'S: 143 Danforth Avenue T: 463-3086

VIENNA HOME BAKERY: 626 Queen Street West T: 703-7278

MIMI'S RESTAURANT: 218 Bathurst Street T: 703-6464

LUNCHTIME

Certain places are all about lunch. In my life, lunch is always at the COFFEE MILL in the Cumberland Terrace. Fabulous in summer around the Oxfam '60s copper orphan sculpture that used to grace the Lothian Mews, it's also superbly cozy inside on a frosty winter afternoon. Order the tuna salad plate if you're hungry; it comes with three mounds of tuna and a horseradishy potato salad – mayo heaven. The busy Hungarian waitress will toss you side plates of buttered rye bread, too, so you can make your own little sandwiches. Yummy cabbage rolls, wiener schnitzel and debreciner as well, though the coffee, unfortunately, sucks. CAKE MASTER, down the street, is for those who don't have a lot of time for lunch. You sit in the narrow below-ground space at absurdly high mini counters for soup made by some little old lady who has been whipping them up every day for years (lentil or broccoli) and virtually any kind of sandwich (try their cheese bread). Lovely lacy chocolate florentines and good coffee, too. More East Bloc action at the uptown **BREAD AND BUTTER** on Mount Pleasant, just above the old Dominion coal silos. It's basically a little neighbourhood cafeteria, with cork-lined trays you can fill with spicy goulash, liptauer or meatloaf sandwiches and a fine apple strudel.

If you find yourself downtown in the corporate jungle at lunchtime, you can avoid the food-court action at two places with some atmo' on pleasantly out-of-it Colborne Street. **CAFE DU MARCHE** is a blandly decorated yet surprisingly authentic French mini-restaurant with excellent quiche, real chicken sandwiches and exquisite gateaux basques. Quick service, too, and good takeout for lunch down the street in the sculpture garden. Virtually next door is **SPINELLO**, an easy place for wood-fired pizza, caprese salad and a satisfying pasta, say, rigatoni or gorgonzola with asparagus or linguine pesto. Like an espresso, lunch can be either very short or very long here, it depends on how much chianti you feel like drinking.

SUSHI BISTRO across from CityTV on Queen Street West is a scene. Packed with overdressed TV types and shoppers wolfing down tuna rolls, the bar feels like a small dose of Melrose. Weird problems do arise here, though: I once had California rolls with rice that was definitely warm. Better sushi, more spanking-clean corporate at Tokyo chain **TAKESUSHI** on Front Street. A tad antiseptic, perhaps, but great salmon, and fast. Funkadelic **O BOY!** on Richmond Street tries a little too hard, but stuffed as it is with kitschy clutter it's a wacky place to go for gooey macaroni and cheese or a humble sandwich. **ACE BAKERY** on King West is an understated bakery/café with only a few tables in its New Age whole-wheat storefront, but they do a mean sandwich on some of their freshly baked breads, say, roasted vegetables and chèvre on focaccia. Nice espresso and fresh juices, too. But sandwich heaven is undoubtedly the adorable original TERRONI on Queen West. Wonderful for its too-extravagant glass chandeliers, multicoloured wall tiles and skinny groovy bar, Terroni cooks up rustic pizzas and seriously arugula-topped bruschetta for rocket fanciers. The sandwich guru here is gifted – no need to be a control freak in this place, just leave the combination de jour up to him. Italian pop tunes, alternately happy and desperately sad, make it hard to leave, long after you've eaten your fill.

My favourite place to spend a Saturday afternoon is CENTRO TRATTORIA FORMAGGI on St. Clair Avenue West. Behind a storefront well hung with prosciutto and provolone, kindly uniformed ladies prepare the daily tavola calda of cannelloni, gnocchi and breaded veal with rapini and roasted potatoes. The few small tables at the back are populated by the regulars: meticulously dressed local retailers and boisterous neighbourhood families. You can pick up your Carapelli olive oil, parmesan and canned San Marzano tomatoes on the way home, too.

COFFEE MILL: 99 Yorkville Avenue T: 920-2108

CAKE MASTER: 128 1/2 Cumberland Street T: 925-2879

BREAD & BUTTER: 507 Mount Pleasant Road T: 488-0036

CAFE DU MARCHE: 45 Colborne Street T: 368-0371

SPINELLO: 53 Colborne Street T: 955-0306

NAMI: 55 Adelaide Street East T: 362-7373

SUSHI BISTRO: 204 Queen Street West T: 971-5315

TAKESUSHI: 22 Front Street West T: 862-1891

OBOY!: 287 Richmond Street West T: 971-5812

ACE BAKERY: 548 King Street West T: 506-1517

TERRONI: 720 Queen Street West T: 504-0320

CENTRO TRATTORIA FORMAGGI: 1224 St. Clair Avenue West T: 656-8111

FANCY LUNCH

When you're lunching with the ladies or perhaps negotiating a three-picture deal, there are a few key places to keep in mind. My fave is the gallery-like **STUDIO CAFE** in the Four Seasons Hotel on Avenue Road. It just feels glam, from the fur-dressed doorman who takes your car in front of the hotel, to the restaurant's brightly lit dividers of pop-coloured sculptural glass. The Studio has a great menu (try the salmon), although, catering as it does to fussy visiting movie stars, the kitchen will prepare whatever you want. Mistresses of shopping love the **HOLT RENFREW CAFE**. It's convenient in-store (third floor) location minimizes any downtime which could be better spent exploring Holt's. And the menu is perfect for chicks – little chèvre-topped salads tossed with balsamic and sandwiches of roasted vegetables. Also, the perfect square room allows for an unimpeded view of newcomers and their outfits.

Everybody loves **BROWNES** on Woodlawn Avenue for its French-looking, heavily lacquered wall, open kitchen and midtown executive/Cineplex-Odeon crowd. Its specialty is rich food with prices to match. In the neighbourhood, the much dowdier **RHODES RESTAURANT** above St. Clair Avenue is better. Get hooked on the horseradish-laced Bloody Marys and juicy burgers and frites or the tangy BBQ chicken salad with nappa and cashews. Best of all, you can park behind, in the city lot on Delisle Avenue, and if you pick up a couple of things from Bruno's, park for free. Fuddy-duddy **LE TROU NORMAND** in Yorkville is still a quaint spot for a long leisurely wine-filled lunch, its old-fashioned French air now honestly earned. The Trou is one of the few places in town to indulge in extravagantly creamy vichysoisse, especially lovely to slurp outside on the tiny patio in summer. Surprisingly good French/Italian food also at neighbouring GILLES BISTRO which is super-cozy in the winter. And the small candlelit and muralled dining room is ideal for licentious behaviour.

The real power brokers who aren't lunching downtown, say, at JUMP or CANOE, can be found trading tales in hunky kitchen artiste Jamie Kennedy's latest haunt, JK ROM at the Royal Ontario Museum. To find the restaurant, you have to walk through the museum to the new wing and the rear little elevator near the Chinese collection. Otherwise, you'll end up lunching in Druxy's on the main floor. You'll know you're in the right place if you find yourself surrounded by well-dressed grey-haired people eating plates of fries – amazing, twice-fried tubers (not greasy, but crisp and made of real potato) that you eat à la Belgique on a wooden platter with a lemony mayo (just for a little extra cholesterol). This lunch will be long, expensive and potentially quite dull, but it's all worth it for the frites.

STUDIO CAFE: Four Seasons Hotel, 21 Avenue Road T: 964-0411

HOLT RENFREW CAFE: Holt Renfrew 50 Bloor Street West T: 922-2333

BROWNES BISTRO: 4 Woodlawn Avenue East T: 924-8132

RHODES RESTAURANT: 1496 Yonge Street T: 968-9315

JUMP: Commerce Court East T: 363-3400

CANOE: TD Tower T: 364-0054

JK ROM: 100 Queen's Park Crescent T: 586-5578

LATE NIGHT

It's really late. Tonight you've driven around endlessly, eaten, drunk, seen a movie, drunk some more, danced, and now you're hungry again. It's definitely past 11:00 p.m., the witching hour for most Toronto restaurants. You really should be going home, but I'll let you in on where you should go, anyway.

PIZZA GIGI for a slice topped with dried chilies.
189 Harbord Street T: 535-4444. Open to 4:00 a.m. every day.

CHRISTINA'S for belly dancers and souvlaki.
535 Danforth Avenue T: 463-4418. Open to 4:00 a.m.
during the week; weekends to 5:00 a.m.

VESTA LUNCH for the city's narrowest lunch
counter that never closes. 474 Dupont Street T: 537-4318.

FRAN'S for banquetburgers and Mrs. Deck's
gold-medal apple pie, round the clock.
20 College Street T: 923-9867.

SAN FRANCESCO for take-out slices and veal sandwiches.
655 Queen Street West T: 703-0335. Open weekends till 3:00 a.m.;
Sunday to Tuesday, to 1:00 a.m.; Wednesday to Thursday, to 2:00 a.m.

PEARL COURT for lobster. 633 Gerrard Street East
T: 463-8778. Open to 4:00 a.m. every day.

cafés

BEST COFFEE

Although you'll find some of the best specialty cups along College Street, it's still possible to go astray. For quality coffee, your best bets are not the nouveau hipster coffeehouses but the less stylish establishments. West of Grace Street, **IL GATTO NERO** is full of smoke and guys arguing vociferously in Italian, just like any good Latino men's social club. Don't be fooled by the cute li'l black kitty outside, this is a macho spot for a serious cup of deep-black espresso, best drunk thick with spoonfuls of sugar. For fluffy cappuccino, walk a block east to the **CAFÉ DIPLOMATICO**. The Dip is a key hangout: outside on summer afternoons, or inside among the signed celeb photos late on a winter night. Good cheap food here, too (slices, pink-sauced pasta, pasta y fagioli), and if you've had enough coffee, try a nutty Amaro Ramazotti over ice.

Trust the couriers, they are serious about their coffee. The young urban nihilist's favourite must be **JET FUEL** on Parliament Street. No regular coffees here, just pierced messengers quaffing giant, surprisingly delicious cappuccinos and wolfing down bran muffins. There's always a buzz in the smoky German expressionist–looking interior. If you're not up to deep thoughts or thrashing music, you may want to get a foamy to go; you can sit 'n sip in the nearby grounds of the exceptionally pretty Necropolis cemetery.

Fans of latte macchiato, the deep rich espresso with just a hint of foam, must be overjoyed now that there are bambini **LETTIERI**. Originally located only in the dreaded Hazelton Lanes, there is

now a second, very charming location on Queen at Spadina, and a Yorkville satellite at Bellair and Cumberland, though at this one, they can't validate your parking stub. Light on true atmosphere, but amazing velvety espresso (and panini and ravioli, too, if you're feeling peckish).

Truly avid coffee snobs may want to check out the importers. Tiny **CUBITA** has a couple of tables in their smart, black-lacquered Yonge Street storefront across from the Metro Resource Library, where you can both sample and purchase the perky Cuban stuff. More of an eye-opener than the Italian variety, this espresso is best drunk short and very sweet. There's always tons of bustle around the efficient **FAEMA** kiosks in the lower level of BCE Place, especially in the mornings when they're besieged by lines of freshly showered working stiffs desperate for a jolt. And since Faema makes the machines, they should know how to work them.

Good morning action at miniature midtown **HAVANA** on Davenport Road, one of the few places in town where you can get a decent café con leche, the smooth Havana-style espresso with a hint of steamed milk. You can flit through *Martha Stewart Living* or *Mirabella* from the magazine rack or sit and stare at passersby through the big picture window. There's also a big-time a.m. lineup at the **COFFEE TREE** in Forest Hill Village, where manicured individuals in expensive casual-wear, pet or child in tow, line up for cups of half-decaf double latte. Bonus: strong regular "Canadian" coffee (especially the Colombian excelso blend) and delicate lemony muffins, too. If you're searching for a great cup of "normal" coffee downtown, try one of the many **MÖVENPICKS**. The excellent Viennese-style coffee at their **MARCHÉ** in the BCE Place foams lightly at the top and is as satisfying as a chocolate bar. The only question is whether you can handle the upscale cafeteria scene – don't they know that when you choose to eat at a restaurant, you might actually want someone to bring things to you?

But when you are about to have a huge day (road trip, moving day), the place for morning java is definitely the classic hoser's donut shop. You know a donut shop has good coffee when there a lot of cabbies stopped out front. At **DONUT WORLD** beside the car wash on Church at Davenport, you can peel in and park in front, seven days a week, twenty-four hours a day, so cabbies frequent. Try it after picking up the necessary supplies at Canadian Tire down the street. Order your coffee regular – hey overdo double-double – and either a French cruller or a fat honey-dip for the full Donut World experience.

IL GATTO NERO: 656 College Street **T:** 531-0543

CAFÉ DIPLOMATICO RESTAURANT AND PIZZERIA: 594 College Street **T:** 534-4634

JET FUEL: 519 Parliament Street **T:** 968-9982

LETTIERI ESPRESSO BAR/CAFÉ: Hazelton Lanes, 87 Avenue Road **T:** 922-8512;

and 441 Queen Street West **T:** 592-1360

FAEMA: BCE Place, 161 Bay Street **T:** 594-9065

CUBITA CAFÉ: 848A Yonge Street **T:** 927-7712

HAVANA: 233 Davenport Road **T:** 968-1097

COFFEE TREE: 431 Spadina Road **T:** 483-BEAN

MÖVENPICK MARCHÉ: BCE Place **T:** 366-8986

DONUT WORLD: 820 Church Street **T:** 964-2189

KEY HANGOUTS

Somewhere cool to waste time is hard to find. Mellow **BAR ITALIA** was the first consciously cool place on College Street and still retains its outré glamour despite its move next door to more glam surroundings and the increased influx of the mini-backpack crowd. The bar up front is perfect for sucking back a quick espresso or Moretti, but most patrons linger at one of the groovy new booths, shooting the breeze over a fluffy cappuccino. If you're uncertain as to whether you should discuss the issues of the day under halogen or simply sink into degeneracy upstairs in the loungy pool-table area, you can always just sit back and eat (yummy antipasto for two, sandwiches bigger than your head, or endive, avocado and bresaola salad). The prettiest of the cafés is undoubtedly **KALENDAR KOFFEE HOUSE** on College Street with its dark Viennese existentialist aura and leaded-glass exterior, but the coffees are only okay here.

Once upon a time a humble Dovercourt corner store, now groovster café, **JOZEF'S 181** is the latest word in coffeehouse-cool. The big thing here is the sandwich-as-art-form, featuring giant sannies named after a strange group of artists (from Warhol to Emily Carr) and made of market-fresh goodies like organic baby greens, colourful peppers and chèvre, all served up in a wry and knowing sort of atmosphere. Good espresso, too, just right for cranking it up on a blasé sort of day.

If there is such a thing as a power-broker coffeehouse, **PATACHOU** on Yonge Street would be it. Typically, the faces obscured behind giant porcelain bowls of café au lait are well maintained, the hair and nails meticulously groomed. Mornings are for Rosedale mothers feeding croissants to their beautifully dressed offspring, notorious property developers slurping café au lait *en bol* and ladies meeting to discuss charitable works. At lunch, the crowd fights for tables, especially on the sunny outdoor patio, where you can wear your Arnets while you pick at your nicoise salad and take delicate sips of Perrier. Pretty little **FRITZ** is a more downtown Italianate version of the same scene. Baby model types in head-to-toe Versace perch in their high chairs to check out the afternoon promenade in the Old York Lanes outside. The drink is espresso, long and sweet, to be consumed with many lipsticked cigarettes and perhaps a calabrese sandwich or pizza rustiche.

Two places where you can actually hang out drinking coffee twenty-four hours a day are the unfortunately named **CAFÉ II CHEZ** and **7 WEST**, both on Charles Street. Mornings are for II Chez, where owner and self-proclaimed coffee guru John McHugh mans the 1961 Gaggia, creating mountainous frothy concoctions for people who wish they weren't awake (writers, film crews and the just badly behaved). The combination of smooth jazz and fine cappuccino seems to soothe their savage breasts. Also a big draw for movie-heads and celebs during the Toronto International Film Festival for the takeout to the Uptown Cinema. Avoid the bland hippie food (scary kidney-bean stews). **7 WEST**, down the street, is sort of a café version of the collegiate Annex pub, the Madison. It, too, comprises three floors of a Victorian house with exposed-brick walls, long bars, pool tables and a packed terrace. Same sort of studenty crowd and anything-goes atmosphere, especially late at night when the scene becomes a bit more "experimental and inspired." Often a lonely-poet type in the corner working on a laptop. The best coffee here is definitely the otherwordly café au lait, and if you have to eat, you're safe with the chili.

The newest thing in the café world seems to be the clothing store-cum-café where the unhip are sorely tested as to whether they should be shopping or sipping. As this tends to weed out the uncertain, you can veg in one of these places in relative solitude. **52 INC.** is on the emerging north side of College before Bathurst. As befits its collegial location, 52 is earnest (hippie clothing and jewelry and Bridgehead coffee), serving up homemade soups and organic snackies with its brew. As its name suggests, **IS**, on Queen West, offers a bit more of the old existentialist blackness, so you can look appropriate hanging at their soda fountain with furrowed brow and a steamy cappuccino in hand. Intellectual jazz fans knock themselves out live here Sunday afternoons.

THE GREEN ROOM, the thespian's hangout of choice, is well hidden, tucked away in an alley behind the Poor Alex theatre on Brunswick Street. Named, of course, for the notorious performers' waiting room, it is a giant space all the better to grandstand in, made comfy with beat-up old furniture and chess sets. Though the place is perilously close to a "Friends" set, it's fun to hang out here sipping a stinky Colombian or attacking their mighty espresso, planning your next move. The Journey's End hotel is an odd location for a hip place, yet the **DAILY EXPRESS** on Bloor Street West survives this accident of birth. Too-smart writers

and refugees from Alliance Française sip, read the café's own newsletter, the *Daily X*, and confess here just off the hotel lobby. Especially Saturday afternoons when the burnt-out crowd is trying to regain their energy.

Now that there's a **FUTURE BAKERY** on virtually every corner offering pierogies in their own unique Ukrainian existentialist atmosphere, it's important to point out that only one of the locations really rocks. The Future on Bloor West, across from the Brunnie, is the heart and soul of the U of T campus, filled as it is with young, intense, cigarette-smoking environmentalists, jaded professorial types and manic scribblers pounding back the java. After a few visits here, you may reconsider your decision to go back to school and help yourself to something slathered in sour cream instead. If your interest, on the other hand, lies more in investigating your sexuality or seeing how the other half lives, you would be better off hanging out at the **SECOND CUP** at Church and Wellesley, the spiritual headquarters of Toronto's gay community. Open twenty-four hours a day seven days a week, this otherwise ordinary franchise is such a focal point that even the steps outside on Church Street are packed with people gabbing over coffee in any weather. Have fun, but in the interest of doing away with a repulsive phenomenon, please refrain from ordering scented brews.

BAR ITALIA: 584 College Street T: 535-3621

JOZEF'S: 181 Dovercourt Road T: 535-5838

KALENDAR KOFFEE HOUSE: 546 College Street T: 923-4138

PATACHOU PATISSERIE: 1095 Yonge Street T: 927-1105

FRITZ: Old York Lane, 138 Cumberland Street T: 966-0111

CAFÉ II CHEZ: 3 Charles Street East T: 968-9078

7 WEST CAFÉ: 7 Charles Street West T: 928-9041

52 INC: 394 College Street T: 960-0334

IS: 894 Queen Street West T: 533-4242

THE GREEN ROOM: 296 Brunswick Street T: 925-7850

DAILY EXPRESS: 280 Bloor Street West T: 944-3225

FUTURE BAKERY AND CAFÉ: 483 Bloor Street West T: 922-5875

SECOND CUP COFFEE COMPANY: 546 Church Street T: 964-2457

BAKERY CAFÉS

Elegant continental **GRANOWSKA** on Roncesvalles Avenue, with its opulent German-made glass display counter, is a choice Polish bakery that once baked bread for the Pope (for his 1983 Downsview airport tour). They make a wicked rum baba, mocha cake or old-fashioned plum-filled jelly donut, grand with their dainty cappuccino. The busy lab-coated salesgirls have an uncanny sense of ethnic heritage: they seem to know when to switch from Polish to English. Rush hour is on weekends and at Easter, and just try to snag a seat outdoors on a sunny Saturday afternoon. Humbler **PETIT PARIS**, really west on Bloor, is best enjoyed in cold weather. Its stuffy old-fashioned rear dining parlour (wood panelling, silk flowers and frilly wall sconces) is great for a hot lunch of schnitzel or cabbage rolls, to be followed up with one of their brilliant danishes, pastries, apple strudel, and, corniest of all, Black Forest cake.

The idiosyncratic **PYRAMID CAKERY** is an oasis. With gaily mismatched Sally Ann chairs, aged walls and giddy Italian pop tunes, this place oozes atmosphere, a reprieve from soul-crushing North Toronto. And, insanely, the delicious cakes are pyramid-shaped (go for the banal-looking, normally shaped coffee cake – it defines "buttery"). Great for a Sunday brunch (try the pierogies) or a soothing coffee break when you're forced to venture north of Eglinton.

Adorably '40s **VIENNA HOME BAKERY** on Queen West is the place to go for wholesome, old-fashioned baked goods like butter tarts or lumpy scones, yummy with the VHB's unpretentious drip coffee. After snacking at the little lunch bar (order a liptauer sandwich), you can always bring home one of their nutty phallic-looking whole-wheat breads. Farther east on Queen is the Estonian bakery **ROONEEM'S**, home to a rather seedy lunch counter but the chewiest, aromatic caraway-laced sweet and sour rye in the city.

The two bustling little bakeries downtown, **DUFFLET** and **ACE**, are primarily in the business of baking extremely delicious and expensive goods for gourmet stores and restaurants throughout the city, but they also have a few in-store tables. Diminutive Queen Street Dufflet is the brain-child of tiny bakerette Dufflet Rosenberg. She does sweet with style; the most mundane of treats, say, a meringue, is given a whole new definition by her vision of baking. King Street Ace Bakery, on the other hand, is all about savoury breadstuffs. Ace specializes in excellent (and costly) baguette and multigrain to go, as well as ambitious prepared sandwiches such as roasted tomato and asiago cheese or roasted red pepper and parmesan on olive bread. And now, Ace does brunch weekends too.

GRANOWSKA'S: 175 Roncesvalles Avenue T: 533-7755

PETIT PARIS CAKE AND COFFEE SHOP: 2384 Bloor Street West T: 769-9881

PYRAMID CAKERY: 2519 Yonge Street T: 489-2246

VIENNA HOME BAKERY: 626 Queen Street West T: 703-7278

ROONEEM'S: 484 Queen Street West T: 504-5205

DUFFLET PASTRIES: 787 Queen Street West T: 504-2870

ACE BAKERY: 548 King Street West T: 506-1517

TEATIME

Going for tea is so out it's in. Almost every large downtown hotel offers afternoon tea, but few of these teas are really worthwhile. Since the demise of the late great Windsor Arms Hotel, the most happening tea is definitely at the **FOUR SEASONS HOTEL** in Yorkville. Here, a fascinating crowd of suits, cosmetic-surgery advocates and socialites on a break from shopping mince words over Earl Grey or Darjeeling, scones and wickedly lardacious clotted cream. A seating tip: if you'd like to engage in serious conversation, avoid being installed near the lobby, as your companion will no doubt be too distracted by the action to fully concentrate. Another lovely tea, very ladylike, is elegantly served in the lobby of the **SUTTON PLACE HOTEL**. Great for stargazing year-round, as tour publicists book either here or at the Four Seasons. A madhouse during the Toronto International Film Festival, perhaps not the best time of year for tea-totalling.

Though the glam **KING EDWARD HOTEL** has much to recommend it (a great spa with wonderful massages, opulent rooms and a wonderfully clubby lobby bar), their tea, while perfectly tasty, is a bit sad and disappointing. It's served off the lobby in a low-ceilinged, mirrored room, and the endless reflection only emphasizes the room's emptiness. If you're going to tea-off downtown, head for the campier **ROYAL YORK HOTEL**. Here you can play Queen Liz for a day; the sumptuously grand gazebos off the Imperial Room are the perfect backdrop to a royally stuffy afternoon tea. And the crustless sandwiches are uncharacteristically fresh.

If you're feeling too manic to sit down, tea sampling at **TEN REN TEAHOUSE** may be appropriate. The Dundas Street headquarters of Hong Kong tea importers, Ten Ren is aromatic with tea and ginseng displayed in official-looking canisters along the walls. The many varieties (try the grape tea) are sampled here daily in a brief yet fulfilling tea ceremony involving many tiny clay pots and vessels. But perhaps what you require is a reading of your leaves. The **ORACLE TEA ROOM**, on St. Clair West, is a fun place for doing just that. Here, you can sit over a pot of tea and glimpse your future in a reading from a trained tea-reading professional, who is also experienced in the ways of tarot card, palm and Egyptian sand readings. Call in advance.

FOUR SEASONS HOTEL: 21 Avenue Road T: 964-0411

SUTTON PLACE HOTEL: 955 Bay Street T: 924-9221

KING EDWARD HOTEL: 37 King Street East T: 863-9700

ROYAL YORK HOTEL: 100 Front Street West T: 368-2511

TEN REN TEAHOUSE: 454 Dundas Street West T: 598-7872

ORACLE TEA ROOM: 596 St. Clair Avenue West T: 653-4648

bars

GET DRUNK

You've just had the most disgusting day imaginable and you call a diehard friend to meet you. You need to be somewhere safe, to soak yourself in liquor (and I mean the hard stuff) and complain bitterly. Go to a hotel bar. That special hotel anonymity (where are you exactly?) seems to accelerate the bonding process. Your best bet is the grande dame – the **LIBRARY BAR** at the Royal York Hotel. It feels like a library; I once found a first edition John McPhee on the shelves. The perfect complements to the perfect birdbath martini: soothing wood veneer, dated (burnt orange) colour scheme, philandering conventioneers, amusing canned Muzak. You can enjoy the waitresses' patented pour from this into the frosty glasses – a sort of wrist flick from which not a drop escapes.

Perhaps the best place to wallow in communal misery is the old **SILVER RAIL**, one of the city's first licensed establishments. There really is a silver rail, and the deep-pink rounded banquettes, too, from the days when drinking was glamorous. It still makes you feel a Lost Weekend coming on, or that maybe Frankie Sinatra is drinking behind you in his skinny Hoboken days. The drinks here are kind of scary – martinis, for instance, are virtually undrinkable (cheap, warm and wet) – but you can catch up on all the latest court room gossip from cops and crowns who are decompressing on bar stools. A place to duck into to get rid of your Eaton Centre headache (the cocktail hour starts whenever you do), or to get in the mood for whatever is on at Massey Hall.

Feel free to try out your favourite off-colour jokes at HY'S, the last stand of the fifty-something white guy. Once again, the drinks aren't great, but the little train-compartment booths have bordello-like sex appeal – red velvet, dark panelling, flocked wallpaper and reproductions of Great Masters. All this suddenly makes you require a stinger. The show is hysterical-boozy standards (Billy Joel to Cole Porter), marimbas and cowbells being plied by the supporting cast (broads in bright lipstick) and on the weekends a bass player who does a mean Elvis impersonation (circa the '68 comeback tour). More of the same at NICKY'S, above EL TORO, plus orange armchairs and a bonus fireplace.

You know they really mean fifty-one floors when you get on the elevator to PANORAMA (formerly AQUARIUS 51) in the Manulife Centre. Once your ears have popped back, look around and you'll find yourself in a time warp of a different kind. It's like a '70s airport lounge up here in the clouds with the other escapees. Go with a group, especially on weekends when the date-night crowd rules. Then you can order weird drinks for one another – this is blenderville, the bartender knows his way around a bottle of Blue Curacao. The 360-degree view is cool and somewhat disorienting, but the real test of your ability to hold on to those frothy drinks is the elevator ride down.

And anytime you must be outside, go only to the ROOFTOP BAR at the Park Plaza Hotel. Why frequent some crummy backyard patio with plastic lanterns, when you can have the whole of the city at your feet? Drinks are expensive, but you're happy to give to the crusty old waiters (one of whom has been lifting trays for half a century). And nosh on the truly addictive warm and salty toasted almonds.

LIBRARY BAR: Royal York Hotel, 100 Front Street West T: 368-2511, ext.2444

SILVER RAIL: 225 Yonge Street T: 368-8697

HY'S STEAK HOUSE RESTAURANT: 73 Richmond Street West T: 364-3326

EL TORO STEAK HOUSE: 39 Colborne Street T: unlisted

PANORAMA: Manulife Centre, 55 Bloor Street West T: 967-5225

ROOFTOP BAR: Park Plaza Hotel, 4 Avenue Road T: 924-5471

MAKE THE SCENE

Right now, these are the places the cool kids go. Still superhot with the film and fashion set (always the fabulous people), **SOUZ DAL** brought cocktails to College Street. The wall finishes may be faux, but the fuzzy, candlelit atmosphere in this tiny room is genuine – poseurs need not apply. The martinis and margaritas (ask for Hornitos premium tequila in this last) are seriously wicked and they have fab olives and pistachios. In the summer, the groovin' back patio is where it's at. Year-round, nobody shows before eleven.

The reincarnation of the short-lived and -loved Lemon, **THE SHAG CLUB FOR MEN**, at Dundas West and Claremont, is the latest thing. Weirdly, Tuesday nights are hopping with a groovy mix – say, the CityTV techie guys beside a buff snowboarding dude passing out those little square invites to a club you've never heard of. Sort of a loud disco lounge with Ben-Hur or Matt Helm mutely projected larger than life and in full Technicolor on the back wall. The hipster patrons are pouring back hard liquor as aggressively as the late Dean Martin. Remember not to lean against the scratchy Astroturf-bearded walls or bean yourself on a stalactite light fixture.

You can go earlier to **COLLEGE STREET BAR**, mainly because you can also eat there (try the red pepper

49

risotto). Sunday nights are particularly happening with live R&B, but any night will find the right people clustered three deep at the bar and visiting one another at all the little tables. Waitresses are always unpleasant, as is the thought of running into everybody you know and fear, or a particularly cretinous arts commentator. Across the street is **SOTTOVOCE**, attached to Trattoria Giancarlo. If you are early enough to find a spot to perch, you can graze here too. Another option on College is the postapocalyptic **TED'S COLLISION**, where most of the time there is funky live music, but occasionally some very young undernourished save-the-environment Teva-sandaled wretches take over for poetry nights (really, shoes with Velcro, need I say more?) and Internet foreplay. But the (generally late-night) arrival of the dread-headed Ted himself means the scene is on.

Now that it's moved to bigger, more fancy digs, **BAR ITALIA** is the scene the cool kids love to diss, but you'll find them paired up here anyway, in droves. The simple decor is a bit too understated, but this is one of the few spots where you can go and get a good long look at lots of cute people. The brightly lit bar has plenty of room for showing off and milling around with a glass of red or a cold Moretti – avoid the nasty martinis. If dining here, stick with the sandwiches and salads of yesteryear. The kitchen is really not up to the pasta and grill menu quite yet. The best thing is the restaurant's name embedded in the terrazzo floor at the door. The worst thing is that there isn't both this place *and* the old Bar Italia.

When in Yorkville, go to either **ENOTECA** or **BLACK AND BLUE** to make the scene. All the beautiful (and/or mighty) people end up around one of these glittery bars in the course of a midtown evening. At **ENOTECA**, sexy Leonardo-style line drawings seem the ideal backdrop to serious wines by the glass, and there's a single-malt list. You can wear a tuxedo without feeling like an idiot, even though everyone else is in jeans. Bonus: they'll stamp your drinks bill for free parking under the Renaissance. At the **BLACK AND BLUE**, the scene is more like a happening private party. Don't venture in if you're anti-smoke, though; this is cigar lovers' heaven, with a smokin' humidor, to boot. More serious drinking goes on in the Provencal-caves film set on Bay Street that is **BISTRO 990**, the spiritual home of the Toronto International Film Festival. The maître d' and bartenders round out the illusion with transitory Parisian accents. The regular fixtures are generally refugees from Sutton Place – writers and producers who live there in the apartments and film types on publicity tours. The cobbled floor is uneven, which only heightens the experience. Still the deal-making zone for motion pictures: the celeb-spotting goes on all year, but come September, when the film festival is on, the upstairs is packed till 4:00 a.m. nightly.

The scene for suits is definitely chef Michael Bonacini's and restaurateur Peter Oliver's two Bay Street corporate outposts. First came **JUMP**, under the old part of Commerce Court East on Wellington: after five o'clock, it's like a mosh pit of working boys (lawyers and brokers) tossing back beers and single malt. The latest, **CANOE**, on the 51st floor of the understated underrated Mies van der Rohe TD Tower is view-HQ of downtown and the lake; on a clear day, you can actually see Rochester, New York. But the overwhelming sense one gets is that everyone is concentrating on the view of action inside. Its two bars encourage some floating around to check out who is there and with whom. Pretty glass-wall-of-leaves thing when you walk in.

Another scene that merits observation is **RODNEY'S OYSTER BAR**. Pick-up and schmooze central, the success of this amusing yet annoyingly packed bar reminds us that people do actually believe oysters are aphrodisiacs. Fab oysters (go for the smallest variety they recommend), best consumed with a dash of vodka and the fresh horseradish. Watch out for the sleazes in the crowd and the bartender with the singularly surly attitude.

Who cares if Latin is but the flavour of the month? It's happening big time on the newest transitional stretch of College west of Spadina at **BARCELONA**. Famed, if only locally, for hosting the jamming Gypsy Kings when they were in town, their fab garage door and appropriately sun-drenched interior, as well as their juicy sangria (betcha can't have just one). The crowd of blasé hipsters into casual spanishing hang out till the wee hours for potential merengue opportunities.

Last call is still always the **CAMERON HOUSE**, in the front room where absolutely everyone who is looking for recognition of one form or another will materialize. Drinks are beers, *en bouteille*, of course, and the crowd of artists, photographers, filmettes and cling-ons who aren't getting any younger mingle in the ever-changing decor. Is it the combined odour of spilled stale beer and inadequate toilet facilities that makes one feel so good to be alive?

SOUZ DAL: 636 College Street T: 537-1883

THE SHAG CLUB FOR MEN: 923 Dundas Street West T: 603-2702

COLLEGE STREET BAR: 574 College Street T: 533-2417

SOTTO VOCE WINE & PASTA BAR: 595 College Street T: 536-4564

TED'S COLLISION AND BODY REPAIR: 573 College Street T: 533-2430

BAR ITALIA: 582 College Street T: 535-3621

ENOTECA: 150 Bloor Street West T: 920-9900

BLACK AND BLUE: 150 Bloor Street West T: 920-9900

BISTRO 990: 990 Bay Street T: 921-9990

JUMP: Commerce Court East, Wellington Street West T: 363-3400

CANOE: TD Tower T: 364-0054

RODNEY'S OYSTER HOUSE: 209 Adelaide Street East T: 363-8105

BARCELONA: 374 College Street T: 967-2867

CAMERON HOUSE: 408 Queen Street West T: 703-0811

HANGOUTS

You hang out in a place because it's in your neighbourhood, or because everybody else you like does, or sometimes just because you can't ever get enough of its peculiar charm. Numero uno hangout is still probably the College Street icon, **BAR ITALIA**, even though they've turned all fancy. You can play pool all afternoon, or share an antipasto *due* or snack at one of the groovy booths. People you know will be there too, whiling away the hours and smoking too many cigarettes. Make a mound of olive pits in your ashtray and before you know it, there's the afternoon.

Next stop is definitely the **CAFÉ DIPLOMATICO** on College Street, renovated and expanded so unstylishly it remains somehow unchanged. Still the best place in town for shamelessly lazy types to sun themselves on the excellent corner patio all summer long, tossing back the airiest cappucino in the city or nursing a lukewarm Ex. Smokes are plentiful at the groovy **LAST STOP CONVENIENCE** across the street, though you can always bum one at the Dip.

Truly hip places generally do not proclaim their hipness right up front, but that's just what the **GYPSY COOP** does, with its cutesy name and sarcastic little boutique area right by the door. I mean, shelves of Kraft dinner and scary votive candles is just a little too self-aware for words. But, the mini-backpack kids are eating it up, earnestly squeezed in here for tea, eats and clever witticisms, at all hours.

The charmingly greasy eternal adman hangout, the **PILOT TAVERN** is hidden away on the fringes of Yorkville. It's easily forgotten, unless of course you're one of the crowd doing old Monty Python routines to another round of Blue. Spiritual home of the patty melt, with sympathetic waitresses and sports on TV, its just like a camp reunion. Somewhat similar vibes at the retro **GEM**, wedged in at the bottom of Wychwood Park on Davenport Road. Great jazzy-bluesy tunes, mellow atmosphere, crowd more theatre-ish. Pleasantly hungover for breakfast.

The Hunt Lounge at **CLINTON'S** is the original hosers' taverne, like you'd find in Montreal. A harshly lit room with rustic log-cabin panelling soaked in beer, this is a quiet, relaxing place to drink. Another safe place is **SQUIRLY'S** on Queen West, which is contemplative and candlelit after noon. In the back patio (closed-in and baseboard-heated all winter), you can hide over your BLT and 50.

The best new thing about the **BEVERLEY TAVERN'S** latest renovation is its garage-door front that opens up in summer. The best old things are the few oversize round tables ideal for group drinking that survived, untouched. The ever-soulful Bev defies trendiness despite its location across the street from the CityTV building. The **360 LEGION**, on the other hand, almost succeeded in removing every bit of true grit in its quest for coolness. Still, it *is* a legion, complete with confused Eastern European waiters and bizarre barbershop chairs. And happily crummy despite a recent overhaul, the **REX HOTEL** on Queen West rocks from its front couches to its teensy but private backroom pool tables. Look for the especially cool Pre-

Madonnas who currently jam every Monday night.

Two great bars so out they're in: **IMPERIAL PUBLIC LIBRARY** at Dundas and Victoria; and **BARRISTERS BAR** at the Hilton Hotel on Richmond Street. The Library is the place to cue up Nat, Frank, Ella and Louis on the nasty old jukebox, make a sloppy scene (or at least break something) or get raunchy in the bathroom. You'll never get the latrine smell out of your clothes. Barristers is a tad more restrained; if you're bored enough, you can always eavesdrop on neighbouring business meetings. The faux English Inns of Courts–studded leather interior, however, can coax messy confessions out of the tightest asses.

BAR ITALIA: 584 College Street T: 535-3621

CAFÉ DIPLOMATICO: 594 College Street T: 534-4637

LAST STOP CONVENIENCE: 596 College Street T: 588-8687

THE GYPSY COOP: 817 Queen Street West T: 703-5069

PILOT TAVERN: 22 Cumberland Street T: 923-5716

GEM BAR & GRILL: 1159 Davenport Road T: 654-1182

HUNT LOUNGE AT CLINTON'S: 693 Bloor Street West T: 535-9541

SQUIRLY'S: 807A Queen Street West T: 594-0574

BEVERLEY TAVERN: 240 Queen Street West T: 598-2434

360 LEGION: 326 Queen Street West T: 593-0840

REX HOTEL: 194 Queen Street West T: 598-2475

IMPERIAL PUBLIC LIBRARY: 58 Dundas Street East T: 977-4667

BARRISTERS BAR: Hilton Hotel, 145 Richmond Street West T: 869-3456

DRINK BEER

Just to remind you why the English pub tradition persists, visit one of the **DUKES** (**KENT**, **GLOUCESTER** or **YORK**, just like in Shakespeare). We all learned to drink here by the foaming pint, and, in desperation, we've all given in to the ploughman's lunch on the menu. This Duke business may seem faux with the dusty red carpets, thick red

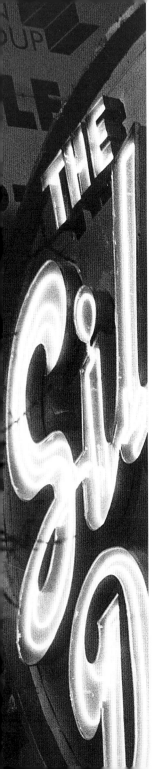

flocked wallpaper and brass rails, but these pubs maintain their integrity because they really are places for talking, smoking and drinking (think thick Double Diamond or Newcastle Brown on tap). Real appropriately seedy English folk use these as their "regular," and add charm and live atmosphere.

The beautiful thing about the **BRUNSWICK HOUSE** is the Felliniesque scene in the backroom. As at any beer hall worth its suds, classic Hungarian waitresses with lace-up skating boots serve watery beer by the tray to frat boys too drunk to care. Glittergran headliner extraordinaire Irene takes the stage and her captive crowd hoots enthusiastically to her special song stylings (such classics as "Obla-dee, Obla-dah"). Sadly, upstairs blues oasis Albert's Hall, once the venue of choice for Bonnie Raitt, B. B. King and a young unknown k. d. lang, is now, weirdly, an off-track betting parlour.

The more discriminating palate should try the beer lists at east end **ALLEN'S** or **CAFÉ BRUSSEL**. Brussel, unsurprisingly, has a vast array of stinky Belgian numbers. And Allen's, just a tad more east on Danforth Avenue, features an encouraging selection of New York State favourites (Rolling Rock, Schaeffer, Genessee). Watch out Tuesday and Saturday when Allen's features potentially frightening Celtic dancers. If you're starved, the burgers (not on the menu) and sweet-potato fries are palatable. Also, a mighty scotch and Irish whisky list and a decent soul and R&B jukebox.

For drinking-game action, pitlike **C'EST WHAT?** has all the classics (Monopoly, Scrabble, Clue, backgammon), and groovier pastimes (Battleship, Crokinole). You might have to listen to a memorably fresh local band named something a little too clever, but you'd be surprised what you can stand when absorbed in Kerplonk.

THE SPOTTED DICK on Bloor Street East is the discerning beer drinker's headquarters for the showoff's bar game of choice – electronic trivia. One of the best things about trivia is that you can select your own nom de plume (perhaps a secret persona), and since the rankings are compared on-screen, you get to gloat privately. The regular crowd goes for the brightly lit bar and the quality setup, and all eyes are focused on the game. The experienced bar staff knows not to ask if you want another Creemore until the round is up. Even if you're a novice, your highly competitive bloodsport instinct takes over and you're hooked. **THE TAP** on Bloor West is a less tense, more casual facility – it's elbows at the bar with baskets of chicken wings and a frosty, stools rockin' to loud Stones. Cool but for the blurry screens and temperamental keyboards. Arguably, the best combination of technology and atmosphere is at the **UNICORN** on Eglinton Avenue, where accomplished trivheads sit in the front section round the fireplace. Play is intense but the vibe is mellow – just try to get one of their gazillion beers on tap in a hurry. Hysterical **PIMBLETT'S** pub is a low-tech, manual salon where you play Trivial Pursuit the old-fashioned way, with die and a board. It's still fun, though, with drag queens as your cheering section, and spotted dogs sniffing you while you drink.

Nice wet drafts, too, at the divey classic, the **MORISSEY TAVERN**. Watch out for the Jarvis and North Toronto teens with fake IDs on weekends, and, of course, the cash-side jar of pickled eggs. But there's Foosball and a cool antique wooden shuffleboard set at the "Mo," and you can watch weird stuff like *Dune* Saturday

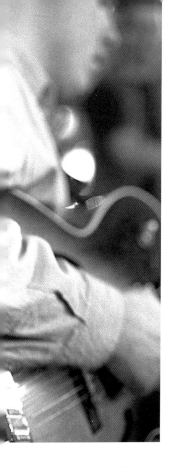

afternoon on the big-screen TV and gradually grow more perplexed.

More kids' stuff at **MADISON** and **PAUPERS** in the Annex. Both playgrounds are three floors of fun with great outdoor decks full of seedy U of T profs, Annex hippies and horny undergrads playing darts. And, best of all, a selection of free phones. Piano bar warning: unless you're interested, avoid the basement of the Madison and the second floor of Paupers. The Mad now has a smoke-free third floor, and a massive new extension to accommodate even more horny undergrads.

The **BLACK BULL** is not only great for biker watching (please note: this is a big hog bar, so don't come screaming up on your Vespa), it also has the best Queen West patio (roomy, on a corner lot, with the key view of the whole strip). Rebel anthems blare from tinny loudspeakers. Waitresses have seen it all and don't put up with any crap. You drink beer in bottles watching Saturday-afternoon drunks round the mini pool table; come nighttime, the air vibrates with the frisson of an incipient brawl. **GROSSMAN'S TAVERN** is moodier, but the bust-ups here might start with broken beer bottles. The legendary beat bar is, however, somewhat of a safe zone because they don't care to change the wrecked-up decor ("decor," in this case, being somewhat of an overstatement).

DUKE OF KENT: 2315 Yonge Street T: 485-9507

DUKE OF GLOUCESTER: 649 Yonge Street T: 961-9704

DUKE OF YORK: 39 Prince Arthur Avenue T: 964-2441

BRUNSWICK HOUSE: 481 Bloor Street West T: 964-2242

ALLEN'S: 143 Danforth Avenue T: 463-3086

CAFÉ BRUSSEL: 786 Broadview Avenue T: 465-7363

C'EST WHAT?: 67 Front Street East T: 867-9499

SPOTTED DICK: 81 Bloor Street East T: 927-0843

THE TAP: 517 Bloor Strret West T: 533-5321

UNICORN: 175 Eglinton Avenue East T: 482-0115

PIMBLETT'S: 263 Gerrard Street East T: 929-9525

MORRISSEY TAVERN: 817 Yonge Street T: 923-6191

MADISON: 14 Madison Avenue T: 927-1722

PAUPERS PUB: 539 Bloor Street West T: 530-1331

BLACK BULL: 298 Queen Street West T: 593-2766

GROSSMAN'S TAVERN: 379 Spadina Avenue T: 977-7000

PLAY POOL

The temple of pool is the aptly named **ACADEMY OF SPHERICAL ARTS**, located in the old Brunswick table factory on Liberty Street. What makes the huge space a scene are the admen and junior record-biz execs here to play serious pool and drink single malts from a serious list among the teeny vignettes of lost-and-found furnishings at salvaged historical tables. It's fun to watch them act unfazed by the challenging arty nudes.

POCKETS 'N SLATES, in a hopeful neon basement in one of the office buildings slated for condo conversion at Yonge and Wellesley, is completely sceneless. All it has, in the unfortunately named (sounds like a cutesy place in Kitsalano) antiseptic quarters are lots of pool tables you can drink at. Actually, its strength *is* its scenelessnesss: the absence of distraction is utterly conducive to playing pool. The crowd is nondescript, too; the only defining factor is a love of the game. Totally different vibes at the **RIVOLI**, which is all about distractions. The Riv is no longer *the* place to meet, or blow your brains out on Laotian food, as it was before pool started to really

happen, but on a rainy weekday afternoon, those pool tables are *the* place to get a solid groove happening. What you get are the tunes you want to hear and enough space between tables to move in and out of the game. Only go to the **DEVIL'S MARTINI** on Simcoe Street right after work, when you can play at the couple of smallish pool tables up front and pretend you're on Canal Street in New York. The tables are small, but they're likely playing the Stones or Skynrd, so all will be copacetic. Later on, there's an over-dressed and over-gelled "bridge-and-tunnel" crowd (just like N.Y!) and hard music that you may find just a bit too fascinating.

Walking into **MYTH** is a nightmare – every head turns. But things get calmer as you make your way toward the pool tables. It's a jumbo space; you feel Lilliputian in the out-size design zone conceived with an eye to special effects. This is the place to go after you've been someplace else, a last stop on your way home (Friday and Saturday nights it's open till 4:00 a.m.). You can wear yourself out here big time with the sensory overload, before you're ready to flop down in front of the infomercials. More restful is **THE COLOURED STONE**, where Nicole Kidman threw her *To Die For* wrap party. Actually, it's kind of an annoying place to play because the floor (stumps set in concrete) isn't even. What it's got going for it is an L.A. feel, a New Age

hush to the room perfect for Zen concentration. Strangely, despite
the quiet, the bartenders seem to be hearing impaired, so just speak
up if you want their attention.

When everything else is closed, practised observers of pool know
there's still **BILLIARDS ACADEMY**, the twenty-four-hour Greektown
acropolis of the game. You and the other strays who can't sleep can
join the waxy habitués with yellowed nails from overtime with
their Player's Lights. Despite their rough look, they *do* suffer fools
gladly. So you needn't necessarily play like Minnesota Fats to end
up here at 3:00 a.m.

ACADEMY OF SPHERICAL ARTS: 38 Hanna Avenue T: 532-2782

POCKETS 'N SLATES: 545 Yonge Street T: 968-7665

RIVOLI: 334 Queen Street West T: 596-1501

DEVIL'S MARTINI: 136 Simcoe Street T: 591-7541

MYTH: 417 Danforth Avenue T: 461-8383

THE COLOURED STONE: 205 Richmond Street West T: 351-8499

BILLIARDS ACADEMY: 485 Danforth Avenue T: 466-9696

GET LAID

ATLAS is largely kids from nice families in expensive casual-wear, trying to pick
up other kids from nice families in expensive casual-wear, though this is second-
best, of course, to going home with one of the skimpily clad model bartendresses.
Absolut must love this place – nobody drinks anything but that and cranberry.
Nice aquarium downstairs and relatively mellow blue and warm-wood design
theme.

The best night MILANO ever knew was the O.J. freeway run, when the disparate
clientele joined together but for a moment, if only as an excuse to pick people up.
Colour-coordinated pool tables and matching purple pinafores on the waitresses
(anorexic model types do best in these) are so unhip they're hurting.

MONTANA is the big ranch-style meat market for twenty-somethings in their first
good suit. No Miss Congeniality prize here – looks are what count. If you're cute
and look willing to laugh at their jokes, you'll get free drinks. Foreplay in this con-
text involves the exchange of business cards.

clubs

LIVE MUSIC

Aggressive vibes at the **HORSESHOE TAVERN**, a venue which is definitely on the macho side of artsy. The slightly wound-up crowd gives attitude that is ardently heterosexual. It all starts with the bouncer, who is kind of mean to you as a rule. And once inside the hot, cramped space, if you want a drink, you have to fight with the bartender and the other patrons showing their balls at the bar. If it's too much, sit at the front bar and ignore the band or jump into the mosh pit stageside. At least you have options. The **RIVOLI** crowd is better-behaved. Its habitués seem to have just discovered Buddhism and beat poetry and are deeply respectful of the jazz-fusion scene. You can see it in their faces – after all, you *are* that close. You're cramped in, concert-style, without the seats.

It's a real bummer when you show up late at the **ORBIT ROOM**. And I miss the former Capriccio for the old black guys playing blues during the Du Maurier Jazz Festival and the corny Trevi fountain mural. Now it's soul and R&B, with excellent martinis and a twinkly starlit ceiling, so we shouldn't complain too much. Sunday night, everybody knows to meet at the **COLLEGE STREET BAR** for the R&B sets. There's always drama over the guy with the big bass, and no one is listening, too busy are they with their relationship dramas. The thing is just to be there. Across the street, **TED'S COLLISION** is for start-up bands, and the collegiate crowd wouldn't know any different. They just wanna get laid.

Visitors to Toronto go berserk over the **BAMBOO** on Queen West – guess us townies are just inured to its Rasta charms. Still, here's where you can dance to the most underrated band in the city, The Satalittes, so we can almost overcome the door's insistence on a jumbo cover, even when you go for dinner. But don't think of going there to eat; this thai is not the pad that Wandee Young used to make before she took off on her own (for Young Thailand I & II). Reggae nights are good for ogling cute dread-headed guys, but really the best scenes are in the bathroom because they're the perfect size for checking out the competition with good primping facilities (large mirrors) too.

The **PHOENIX** on Sherbourne Street rocks Sundays with heavy-duty metal and '80s retro night. For live bands, it's the ideal place – intimate but with lots of space for expressive dancing. Check the models working off roast beef dinners! Of late, this is where Courtney Love dove into the pit and lost her bracelet in the crowd, and Chrissie Hynde and Patti Smith both looked skinny and raw. It's also, of course, the reincarnation of the eternally rocking late lamented Diamond Club, where in the '80s everyone did wads of coke in the bathrooms and danced their heads off to Devo. Recently, indie heroes Superchunk brought down the house; but the problem is, in the '90s, this is also where you come to see cornflake girl Tori Amos.

The much graffito-ed **LEE'S PALACE** on Bloor West is a two-story, multidisciplinary funhouse. You can sit at the bar and listen to the band from a distance or gab with your friends in the mezzanine or sit around the stage or toss yourself into the fray stageside. Decent capacity downstairs so you get some big names in an up-close-and-personal setting; the weirder (read: less practised) bands play upstairs. You can get lucky here – I once saw Daniel Lanois come onstage to do a surprise jam with angst-driven Junkhouse. Unbelievably groovy.

The backroom at the **CAMERON HOUSE** always features good local acts, like Tom Davis and the Beatnik Beats – you know, the sideburn guy with the black T-shirt. Even though you could hardly find this room inspiring, it seems that the bands that play at the Cameron define the moment. Real devotees and hopeful groupie types sit entranced at the front, on the floor.

The classic hotel/tavern, the **GLADSTONE** was way-cool before Queen that far west happened. In the Cameron vein, with smelly Polish sculptors and bald actors hanging on to their bottles of Blue for dear life, complaining biliously to people who aren't even listening. Now, it's all about indie bands and the groovier of OCA's student bodies. Down College Street, at Bathurst, the tangy orange velour curtain in the front window is so fabulous at **LOLA'S LOUNGE**, I can bear (but only briefly) the youngsters earnestly grooving to acid jazz.

More cerebral types should check out **GATE 403**, a cool gallery cum performance space for live jazz and blues way out on Roncesvalles. No thrashing about here, rather deep and knowing musical appreciation with appropriate body movements (nodding head, finger snapping, etc.). The Gate hosts visiting bright lights of varying abilities, so call first or otherwise run the risk of being subjected to the truly haunting strains of one of our exceptionally mediocre local divas. Same scene at the tiny upstairs **TOP O' THE SENATOR**, a lounged-up attic above the old Senator restaurant on Victoria Street. Here, earnest appreciation rules for the typically youngish clientele in blue velvet drinking cognac into the night.

THE MATADOR is the place you go when its late but you're not ready to go home. You may well see the band you saw elsewhere earlier that night, now doing double duty as a country act. It's kind of sexy to dance country-style drunkenly with weirdly serious folk in full TNN regalia. Look for the shady station wagon in the parking lot out back to buy your mickey (this late-night place serves no booze).

HORSESHOE TAVERN: 370 Queen Street West T: 598-4753

RIVOLI: 332 Queen Street West T: 596-1908

ORBIT ROOM: 580A College Street T 535-0613

COLLEGE STREET BAR: 574 College Street T: 533-2417

TED'S COLLISION & BODY REPAIR: 573 College Street T: 533-2430

BAMBOO: 312 Queen Street West T: 593-5771

PHOENIX: 410 Sherbourne Street T: 323-1896

LEE'S PALACE: 529 Bloor Street West T: 532-1598

THE REX: 194 Queen Street West T: 598-2475

GLADSTONE HOTEL: 1214 Queen Street West T: 531-4635

LOLA'S LOUNGE: 426 College Street T: 921-9400

GATE 403: 403 Roncesvalles Avenue T: 588-2930

TOP O' THE SENATOR: 249 Victoria Street T: 364-7515

THE MATADOR: 466 Dovercourt T: 533-9311

DANCE JOINTS

By definition, the "dance club" is wildly unhip. The lineups are stacked with tacky suburbanites covered in lipstick and coated in hairspray. Not to mention that lining up is inherently uncool. But there are some nights when you want to feel the beat of the bass in your solar plexus and sweat with strangers.

The best place to do this right now is **EL CONVENTO RICO**, a gay Latino nightclub in a College Street basement across from the Miracle Mart. The things that I love about this club: the fact that you drink cuba libres; the old Havana/Miami Beach kind of photographer guy who takes Polaroids of your party for two dollars; the crowd on the dance floor knows how to merengue and perform all the initials in "YMCA"; let alone the moving drag show (sometime after 1:00 a.m.) straight out of the opening scene in *Priscilla, Queen of the Desert*. Another gay cabaret/dance club (this one with a comedy element) excellent for shaking that groove thang is **TALLULAH'S**, a staple of the Church and Wellesley scene. Wild dancing starts after the shows, around midnight. Excellent for just plain dancing as it's totally without pretensions or inhibitions, not even a cover.

Now, the following places are more hard-core mainstream discotheques. When there's a good band, **RPM** and sister club the **WAREHOUSE**, at the foot of Jarvis Street, have always offered enough

67

ballroom space for dancing big time. It's traditionally really dark inside, and ergonomically correct, with a centre bar in the middle of the action. But now that fancy-club owner Charles Khabouth has his hands on it, it's hard to say what the groove will be like.

WHISKEY SAIGON on Richmond Street is downtown CFNY central: deejay Maie Pauts live Thursdays; and the live show "Retro Radio '80s" Sundays with Martin Streek. Oversize, kind of terrifying three floors of dancing fools. And Saturday nights, lines of listeners outside waiting to join the party. The grossly named **FLUID** on Richmond Street was once Stilife, another inappropriately named dance place. This space went from industrial overload (like a '30s cruise ship), to baroque madness, to its current state of overdecoration, with exaggerated shapely forms and jarring colours. Sundays, deejays Dave Campbell and Paul E. Lopez spin Meat Market (and I thought that was every night). The blue-lit **ORCHID** on Adelaide is another hyper-decorated environment stuffed with arrivistes. The really funny thing is the cordoned-off VIP room, the "champagne" lounge with its phallic leopard-skin flotation device that is completely visible to lesser beings. Another Stilife spinoff, **IVORY** (by executive producer Charles Khabouth) is still about being on the guest list. Like we really care to be among the hard-living Yorkville Kato Kaelins in the crowd, though the exotic boudoir decor has a certain soigné appeal.

The newest additions to the local club scene are the giant, stylized **JOKER** and the new Satellite Lounge upstairs at the wildly popular

ATLAS BAR & GRILL. The Satellite Lounge has the appropriate starlit ceiling, an ovoid bar about which the painstakingly coiffed dance to "old school" (everything from the Supremes to '80s dance hits). Another sign that they know our hot buttons here: the Satellite caters to the big stogie trend with a giant lit glass humidor as wall decor. The nightmarish **JOKER** is all about size, a $1.2 million super-club jammed with supermodel wannabes in the appropriate harlequin-style setting. But talk about '90s – the main floor is devoted entirely to surfing the Internet. Dancing (to retro '80s tunes) happens on the churchlike faux-vaulted third floor.

Mostly kids in slouchy trousers at Adelaide Street's **POWER BAR** waiting for the Raptors to arrive. Lots of blondes hanging off shaven-headed black guys with goatees, especially on Hi NRG Fridays and Saturdays. Good wall-of-mirror idea, although cheaply executed, and the see-through floor is vaguely disorienting. Two blocks down, on Adelaide, the upper walkway at **LIMELIGHT** allows you to look through to the sweaty teens in dry ice. Regulars know to wear white for black-light visibility. **OZ** and **EMERALD CITY** on Mercer Street are for kids who arrive home late and drunk with a voice hoarse from screaming.

EL CONVENTO RICO: 750 College Street T: 588-7800

TALLULAH'S: 12 Alexander Street T: 975-8555

RPM/WAREHOUSE: 1 Jarvis Street T: 869-0045

WHISKEY SAIGON: 250 Richmond Street West T: 593-4646

FLUID LOUNGE: 217 Richmond Street West T: 593-6116

ORCHID: 117 Peter Street T: 598-4990

IVORY: 69 Yorkville Avenue T: 927-9929

ATLAS: 129 Peter Street T: 977-7544

JOKER: 318 Richmond Street West T: 598-1313

POWER BAR: 230 Adelaide Street West T: 977-1731

LIMELIGHT: 250 Adelaide Street West T: 593-6126

OZ & EMERALD CITY: 15 Mercer Street T: 506-TOTO

shopping

CLOTHING

Now that your mother doesn't shop for you anymore, drop the distinction between work- and play-wear. All you really need are a few great pieces – tops, pants, jackets – to wear until they die. Since you're going to sport these essentials everywhere, invest in quality up front – nothing is nastier than a pilly sweater or a shiny jacket.

Even though **GAP** is looking a little preppy now, what with its competition, **CLUB MONACO** and **ROOTS**, getting groovier by the minute, it always has cheap versions of the garment you need – a ribbed black turtleneck, a skimpy satin slip-dress, mix 'n match bikinis, twinsets in every colour of the rainbow, big cozy crewnecks and of course, the single-pocket tee. But don't go there for jeans – the uptight, mannish Nantucket cuts don't look good on women.

More stylish (more expensive) big sister to **GAP**, the **BANANA REPUBLIC** look says, "I have a great job." Nice soft-styled women's suits à la Emporio Armani, and truly great men's weekend-wear handsomely displayed in their old bankhall-like Bloor Street store. Jeans, tees, underwear, jewelry to complete the look (love the guys' ties), even a body-care line with excellent soap (try the white flower).

In the '80s, tourists came to **ROOTS** for the Canuck logos and quality leather goods, and visiting celebrities came to be photographed in their sportif jackets (gallery showing on permanent display at the Avenue Road store). Today, Roots is all about relaxed, sophisticated, affordable separates key to any wardrobe – you could be wearing one of their simple tees with a pair of jeans in the airport in Paris and still feel pretty cute. And, it's great for cozy, tactile fabrics (pique, waffle, sherpa fleece). Also, amazing indestructible kids' clothes with the right aesthetic: gingham, clear colours, simple styling. Fall '96 marks the launch of the Roots Home line, the same concept taken to linens and accessories.

Currently poised to conquer New York, **CLUB MONACO** already has us under their spell. These guys are sexy and of-the-moment and they just don't miss: from the key black cigarette pant to the perfect pea-coat, to keep us coming back for more. Which is, of course, the strategy. Every week, new must-have clothes are carefully stacked on the shelves and hung on the racks by the comely CM-clad saleskids, who are all completely converted to the cause.

I think there are people in this city who actually live at **HOLT'S**. It all starts with the ever-charming doorman, Tom Hargitai, elegantly clad in all kinds of weather (his furry winter ensemble is the most flattering). He does a very good job of convincing you that he knows who you are. The glam main floor is for Emporio Armani, Chanel makeup, Annick Goutal perfume, Gucci, hats, bags, glasses, scarves and baubles (check the fun vintage jewel case from Carol Tannenbaum's rotating collection). Lower level is all boys' stuff, from Katharine Hamnett to Armani and Holt's private label, from shirts to suits. The second floor is where you can watch fashion victims

eyeing Brown's shoe treasures and scan the design heavies for grown-up girls (Donna Karan, Jil Sander, Calvin Klein). Style hounds first case the wacky Cachet boutique (Anna Sui, Gaultier, Helmut Lang, Zelda, Ghost), desperate individuals flip anxiously through the racks of party dresses and nobody can ignore the essential lingerie department, especially since it's on the way to the most fabulous glittering and marbled public washrooms in the city. The top floor is for Holt's private-label suits and separates, which are always great knockoffs (currently, Mamie Eisenhower suits, Parallele-style synthetic disco shirts and sleek ski pants) and cheaper groovster labels like CK, DKNY and RL (at these prices, you get only the initials). Also a few home goodies and the marvelously convenient third-floor Holt Renfrew Cafe.

Smaller, uptown **IRA BERG** is a select, just-for-women mini-department store that used to be too scary to walk into (the school mistress-variety sales staff peering disapprovingly down their bi-focals at you, their "Can I help you?" implying that the task would certainly be beyond them). Now worth a visit for its alternatif offerings: Dries van Noten, Paul Smith, DKNY, TSE 'shmeres, red-hot JP Todd driving mocs and Kiehl's cosmetics. You can find party stuff here, too, some of it even affordable, like swingy little dresses by Tocca and Betsey Johnson and chic bags by Prada's poor relation, Granello. The delicate little building with its sweeping staircase looks like a couture house out of a '50s *Vogue*, and you can park in the lot behind.

GAP: 60 Bloor Street West T: 921-2225; plus 10 other Toronto locations

BANANA REPUBLIC: 80 Bloor Street West T: 515-0018; plus 3 other Toronto locations

ROOTS: 195 Avenue Road T: 927-8585; plus 15 other Toronto locations

CLUB MONACO: 403 Queen Street West T: 979-5633; plus 24 other Toronto locations

HOLT RENFREW: 50 Bloor Street West T: 922-2333; plus Yorkdale and Sherway Gardens

IRA BERG: 1510 Yonge Street T: 922-9100

JEAN JOINTS

When all you want is a plain old pair of baggy button-front Levi's to live in, go to **WINGATE'S**. This is the classic Yonge Street storefront jeans store with jaded yet patient staff who will kindly let you start with the size 4's and work your way into reality. And, coming out of the change room for the seventh time, you may rub shoulders with a prominent baseball or hockey jock in his underwear.

For jeans that make more of a statement, try the Danforth, east of Broadview, where side by side are two great jeans stores with all the fab labels. The cutest is **MOTOR OIL**, a sort of Indiana Hoosier Kmart from the '30s. Instead of GWGs, they carry more cerebral jeans by Italian labels Rivet, Replay and weird Hollywood Ranch (Japanese designer Gen Tarumi claims he dreams these up tripping on acid). The charming continental owner, Robert Celsi, offers encouraging remarks about your butt when you venture out of the change room (almost makes the 200 bucks you drop here for a pair of jeans worthwhile). Down the street is **BODY BLUE**, a bit more pedestrian, but some great stuff – jeans by Big Star, Replay, Guess and CK, and ruff 'n tough leathers from Indian Motorcycle.

The toque-hatted hip-hop crowd shells out some bucks for their low-slung jailin' trou by labels like Fuct, Stussy and X-girl at **UNCLE OTIS** in Yorkville. Maybe its the mini-mall location (just like in L.A.) that inspires. Around the corner, they can complete their ensembles at RED OR DEAD, the chichi London Camden Market line of fascinating footwear, with some fab house-label and Diesel items for above the ankle (anyone for a pacifier-toggled pink plush duffle coat?). Local hip-hop designers TOO BLACK GUYS have their atelier just off Bathurst Street in the Annex. A destination for out-of-town deejay types, Too Black Guys is especially good for politically outraged T-shirts and a brilliant oversize hockey sweater that's jammin' on a sista. Similar 'tude is on for little groovsters around the corner at SOUL KIDS.

Less gangsta more kinda mod-street looks are the thing at NO. 6 on Queen Street West. Mostly for men (of the liberated-from-a-regular-job variety), they've got cool threads like super-skinny black stretch Beatle jeans, white leather jackets, slightly ugly stripey jerseys and stuff from Paul Smith, like a poet's shirt of fuzzy towelette. Same story at nearby NOISE, which could be a reference to the tunes they play. Requisite big, black hefty postie boots here too. Farther west on Queen is the extremely hip HEAVENLY, with its indie girl-band looks, like shrunken tees sporting brownie badges and beaded macramé handbags. The super-cool salespeople sport that completely disinterested look, sprawled on the couch doing macramé to Wayne Newton.

Along Kensington Avenue in the market, mixed in between the used-clothing meccas like COURAGE MY LOVE and EXILE (which, incidentally, offer racks upon racks of used jeans), there are a few spots selling funky new stuff, all fairly cheap. The prettiest is LILITH'S GARDEN, with its eccentric skateboard-cum-mosaic-relic interior. The thing here right now is heavy polyester clash glam grunge.

WINGATE'S: 538 Yonge Street T: 922-9156

MOTOR OIL: 239 Danforth Avenue T: 466-4038

BODY BLUE: 201 Danforth Avenue T: 778-7601

UNCLE OTIS: 26 Bellair Street T: 920-2281
RED OR DEAD: 84 Yorkville Avenue T: 929-6432; 427 Queen Street West 340-8123
TOO BLACK GUYS: 2 Follis Avenue T: 538-3451
SOUL KIDS: 984 Bathurst Street T: 535-3861
NO.6: 290A Queen Street West T: 593-2745
NOISE: 275 Queen Street West T: 971-6479
HEAVENLY: 779 Queen Street West
COURAGE MY LOVE: 14 Kensington Avenue T: 979-1992
EXILE: 20 Kensington Avenue T: 596-0827
LILITH'S GARDEN: 15 Kensington Avenue T: 591-6800

FABULOUS OUTFITS

Neither man nor woman can live by black T-shirt alone. Sometimes a bit more is required. If Holt's doesn't have your special thing, it may be calling out for you in one of the city's fancier boutiques. **290 ION** on Queen Street West is a perfect little boutique: a women's store with the latest from less mainstream designers like Zelda or Betsey Johnson and local young stars like Lida Baday, Joyce Gunhouse and Judy Cornish (Comrags) and Mimi Bizjak. Dresses, as well as more adventurous suitings that may appeal to those gunning for control at the office. Hyper-stylish jackets and separates by Big Fish are the rule at neighbouring **PARADE**, which might have chic evening looks as well (long bias-cut skirts and '40s-inspired tuxedos), but watch out for the crabby owner.

Behind the Hollywoody John Street mural, **PRICE ROMAN'S** husband-and-wife design team (Derek Price and Tess Roman) flog their own fine women's jackets, skirts and pants. For a more special event, glam frocks for parties and hip weddings are available off the rack or by custom order at **LOWON POPE DESIGN**. In the relaxed studio of yet another romantically involved design duo, lovely Lana Lowon and her husband, Jim Pope, you may see just the thing or, even more fabulous, have it made for you.

More pretty dresses, Cal-modern jackets and such at uptown **EMROOZ**, which is easy to forget about with its unfortunate Yonge and Egg location, and yet important to remember for something affordable and a little different. Same story at **VENNI**, which, though a sort of chain place, has a few good cheap pieces you can always use to freshen up your look, usually in the work-through-evening category.

Wacky **F/X** is always party central with edgy clothes from House of Field, Norma Kamali, Anna Sui and Maxfield that put you in the mood for a good time. From corsets to giant flowered hats to furry sunglasses, F/X stocks all the party tricks. Now with stores on Queen, Spadina and in Yorkville (we can't wait to see how the plastic-flower-strewn exterior holds up), all occasionally graced with the strange-yet-adorable Simon as Borscht Belt emcee. Paris-born **KOOKAI** is a Yorkville neighbour with tiny, perfect funky clothes for the tiny, perfect and funky. Right now it's orange patent high-heeled Gucci knockoffs, stretch plaid jumpers and a super-freaky silver shearling jacket great for any fan of Rick James.

For soft, flowing and romantic party-wear, check out the **IRISH SHOP**, strangely stocked with both avant-garde retro-inspired designs from Ireland and amusingly straight items like Celtic friendship rings and tweedy poet's jackets. Extremely helpful and terminally cheery Irish ladies wait tirelessly on you as you fret over whether the cream chiffon is too sheer.

If you're looking for something really soupy, along the lines of a rubber bodysuit or leopard vinyl halter dress to make an entrance on the dance floor at, say, Venus or Orchid,

perhaps you're better off shopping at the divinely tacky Yonge Street stores. **KINGDOM**, at Charles Street, specializes in kinky silver-lamé slips to wear with biker jackets and fascinating new forms of Lycra. Down the street at Wellesley is **SHKANK**, excellent for its yicky name and wild club-wear for guys and gals. Owner Nina and her boys are up nights sewing new and weirder forms of PVC weekly.

Recent subscribers to Cher's new Goth-wear catalogue needn't send away, they can stock up on all the key Satanic-vixen looks in club-wear at **FASHION CRIMES** on Queen Street West, where designer Pam Chorley has always had a thing for velvets. From lace-up bodice Empire-waisted baby-doll confections, to natty wine-coloured Edwardian morning coats, she has the look covered. And now that Pam's into babies, there are biker jackets in teeny sizes for toddling sirens in training.

To convey your world-weary, slightly morose refinement, you'll need to spend a lot for a complicated cerebral Japanese design. You can find the best of Comme des Garçons, Matsuda, Yohji Yamamoto and Issey Miyake at either **MARI** or **YUSHI**, a stone's throw away from each other in Yorkville. This consistently means strong sculptural effects with interesting fabric action (wrapping, pleating or textured weaves) and little or no colour. These clothes are guaranteed to be either virtually unnoticeable (so terribly chic) or to make a huge statement.

290 ION: 290 Queen Street West T: 596-7296

PRICE ROMAN: 267 Queen Street West T: 979-7363

LOWON POPE DESIGN: 692 Queen Street West T: 504-8150

EMROOZ: 2027 Yonge Street T: 481-2282

VENNI: 274 Queen Street West T: 597-9360; plus 2 other Toronto locations

PARADE: 557 Queen Street West 868-6789

F/X: 391 Queen Street West T: 585-9568; 116 Cumberland Street, T: 975-5511;

152 Spadina Avenue T: 703-5595

KOOKAI: 97 Yorkville Avenue T: 966-3878

IRISH SHOP: 110 Bloor Street West T: 922-9400

KINGDOM: 687 Yonge Street T: 960-3643

SHKANK: 672 Yonge Street T: 515-0959

FASHION CRIMES: 395 Queen Street West T: 592-9001

YUSHI: 162 Cumberland Street T: 923-9874

MARI: 132 Yorkville Avenue T: 961-1302

SHOES

Have you noticed that you can always be in the mood to buy a pair of shoes? They're cheaper than a new car, and even if you're feeling fat, at least your feet haven't changed size. But if you're hobbling along on a pair of worn-down heels, or if every pair of shoes in your closet looks dead wrong, the first place to head is **BROWN'S**. They always have what you need, from the perfect little black boot to a dressy Donna Karan mule. Skip the Eaton Centre altogether, the kiosk at Holt Renfrew is a convenience thing, but the best Brown's location is definitely the one on the ground-floor level of Hazelton Lanes. A word of warning: this store is well-attended by other people who read fashion magazines, so if you want the shoe of the season in a size 8, get there early.

Don't be frightened off by the tall, lithe, Italian game-show sales staff at **CORBO BOUTIQUE** on Bloor West. March right in and try on the wares of the ultimate shoe fetishist, Manolo Blahnik, for a little number by Michel Perry,

Stefan Kelian or Robert Clergerie. The shoe as abstract art, but here, unlike at the Bata Shoe Museum, you get to take them home. Also great clothes by the fab Italian label Industria, Katherine Hamnett, Costume Nationale and stretch-meister Liza Bruce. If dropping a cool $400 for a pair of shoes makes you a tad nervous, you can also check out their cheaper and cheerful annex, **CORBO STUDIO** on Cumberland, for "younger" lines like Seducta, Kelian Studio and Espace. Neat rags, too: sexy low-rise sailor-front pants and heavy rayon shirts from design sensation Parallele, Gauthier jeans and Katherine Hamnett jeans.

Another Yorkville shoe HQ is **DAVID'S**, typically the first stop for the ladies-who-lunch set searching for the perfect appliquéd suede flat. It's still worth looking into, for the Charles Jourdan numbers and the less committed shoes in their new annex, **CAPE DAVID**. For showstoppers, though, go around the corner to the new Yorkville location of **RED OR DEAD**. They seem to consistently carry the shoe you simply must have, just because it's so amusing. And, at $120 a pair, it's no major investment. Pretty private-label bags, jackets and pants, and Diesel, too.

If you want the latest in shoes, but are afraid to go all the way (are wedgies forever?), you had best check out **PEGABO**. All over town, from Bloor Street to the Eaton Centre, they have stylish, cheap shoes for men and women under their own label. Lately, they've become so good at knocking off the trends, you find yourself with too many options. And there's something pleasantly democratic about the crowd – everyone shops here, from preteens on an allowance to furtive careerists.

For serious boys' shoes, the kind you would wear with a suit, there are really only a couple of choices. First stop would be the main floor at **HOLT'S** for the To Boot and Kenneth Cole stuff that puts a sparkle in the eye of any frustrated i-banker. For stuffy old brogues, there's always **DACK'S**, the Bay Street boys' pick for durable, well-made shoes (from Church's of England as well as their own brand). Since they haven't updated their look for years, there are still some deeply amusing doozies on the shelves, like a slim '60s croc model, perfect for Dick van Dyke, as well as a few lizard Miami Beach numbers with a snazzy Cuban heel.

For clunkier footwear, try either Yonge Street at Wellesley or Queen at Spadina. Both strips are filled with shops selling Doc Martens and other AirWares. The best little Yonge Street spot is probably **D & M CLEARANCE**, which has the added attraction of stocking a few out-of-date and discontinued models that can still cause a commotion. More Docs, Terra Wild Siders, adorable Geronimo's and cloggy things by Sam and Libby at hippie hangout **GET OUT SIDE** on Queen Street. If only you could get service from the pierced kids playing hacky sack at the cash. Farther west is the **AUSTRALIAN BOOT COMPANY**, the only place in town to buy the studly Blundstone boot. "Blunnies" are amazing because they always manage to look right, even though they give you platypus feet.

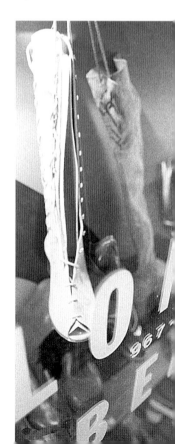

At **YOUNG CANADA** they've been measuring squirming little kiddie feet on those sliding metal rule things for forty-five years. All the traditional school shoes are here, from Rite Step and Bonnie Doon, as well as simple Keds and proper black-patent party shoes. What's more, kids get balloons on their way out, custom-filled from the battered helium tank near the cash by the kind but vaguely harassed-looking sales staff. **PETIT PIED** is sort of the Corbo for kids. They have tiny versions of the most modish footwear, from a tiny patent-leather go-go boot, to the classic English school shoe by Start Rite (shoemaker to the Royal Family). The crowd of well-dressed whiny offspring is catered to with patience and some humour.

BROWN'S: Eaton Centre T: 979-9270 ; plus 10 other Toronto locations

CORBO BOUTIQUE: 131 Bloor Street West T: 928-0954

CORBO'S STUDIO: 162 Cumberland Avenue T: 966-8784

DAVID'S: 66 Bloor Street West T: 920-1000

RED OR DEAD: 84 Yorkville Avenue T: 929-6432;

427 Queen Street West T: 340-8123

PEGABO: 778 Yonge Street T: 928-1213; plus 5 other Toronto locations

HOLT RENFREW: 50 Bloor Street T: 922-2333

DACK'S: 101 Richmond Street West T: 368-0771; plus 7 other Toronto locations

D & M CLEARANCE: 566 Yonge Street T: 967-1711

GET OUT SIDE: 437 Queen Street West T: 593-5598

AUSTRALIAN BOOT COMPANY: 791 Queen Street West T: 504-2411

YOUNG CANADA: 523 Eglinton Avenue West T: 483-2233

PETIT PIED: 890 Yonge Street T: 963-5925

STUFF

Shoes aside, fulfillment can be found in the quest for great stuff. You know, *fabulous* trinkets: bed linens, candlesticks, mirrors, stationery, not to mention the odd chaise longue. Even if your own humble digs have a long way to go, you can still fantasize, fuelled by a furtive reading of Martha Stewart.

For the latest word in the glittery stuff shelter magazines are made of, go to Queen Street, west of Spadina. First stop is **DU VERRE**, giftie central, with its often edgily esoteric or whimsically shaped stock of lamps, 'sticks, pillows, boxes and frames. Currently, the mood here is dreamy moderne: green-glass oyster-shell plates rimmed in gold, boxes of goatskin parchment and brilliant tasseled-silk pendant fixtures. **URBAN MODE** is more funky practicality, with shiny barbershop-inspired chrome Italian canisters, court jester furniture, fat chenille throws, classy Scandinavian tableware and the world according to Umbra (the ultra-trendy rod-and-frame people).

Round the corner on Beverley Street is **UP COUNTRY**, the giant new multilevel temple to the bourgeois lifestyle. Thirty thousand square feet of arts and crafts and Mission style, plus classic oversize furniture, slipcovered in slightly messy washed neutral cottons and urban-naif Provence-inspired metalwork. Local heroes are also showcased: the moody handiwork of Celtic gesso artiste Teresa Casey, as well as tiny environmentally friendly table treats from the clever boys at Harvest Gifts. The feeling is less *Elle Decor* than *House Beautiful*, but in a space as large as this, as in ABC Carpets & Home in New York, you're sure to find some little trinket you just can't bear to live without.

Across the street is the gallery-like **20TH CENTURY**, where the beauty goods of the last few decades await new owners. Chairs by Eames, teak by Jensen, cool crisp Scandinavian blown glass, perfect for display in your Diva-style garage loft. More of the same, slightly less perfect Aalto chairs and Noguchi lamps at **QUASIMODO**, farther west on Queen.

If you're looking for something a bit less rarefied, a lot more rugged, try the Indonesian importer **JALAN** for its vigorous collection of artfully battered teak armoires and artifacts (wooden signs and temple carvings). Iron is the primary element across the street at **PAVILION**, crammed with hand-wrought beds, lamps, drapery rods and coffee tables with legs of curlicued, raw or patinated iron, as well as highly romantic pillows and linens.

Come up for air at the esoteric **JAPANESE PAPER PLACE**, which is an endlessly entertaining art resource as well as a shopping adventure. To get off on these super-subtle handmade Japanese papers and delicate paper constructions and cards, you've got to appreciate their delicacy. Once you do, you'll find yourself buying more than you'll ever need. Same story at the neighbouring Japanese ribbon and trim shop **MOKUBA**, which displays its awesome collection of 17,000-odd items in a handsome converted bank. If you can't find the perfect ribbon here, you may as well give it up.

Another fun design district to browse in is King Street East. First stop is the so-very-French **TRIANON**, which really belongs in the sixth arrondissement, say, on the rue Jacob. Inside are astounding impractical lamps with shades of preserved roses on thorny gilded stems, a mottled silverleaf pear topped with a leaf of organza and beautiful silk upholstered French chairs. Nearby **L.A. DESIGNS** is a bit less together. They've used the shotgun approach to retail – throw all kinds of stuff into the showroom to see what sticks. Some good stuff here, like the classic Parisian café–style rattan bistro chairs plus all the finishing touches imaginable. If you've been longing for a coral Georgian manse CD tower, you'll find it here.

For pieces that transport you to another, more poetic world, visit atmospheric **507 ANTIQUES** in a brick warehouse on Carroll Street. This ethereal treasure trove is largely a decorator's secret. You'll find it full of glorious weathered statuary and relics for the garden (stony creatures and architectural fragments of iron or wood) which, when used indoors, add a pleasing, melancholic aura.

Charming **L'ATELIER** at Yonge and Summerhill is a tasteful oasis of antique and reproduction furniture and objets d'art from a kinder era, say a bronze crown, or crested pillows of Scalamandie silk or a Victorian apothecary globe. Owner Yussef Hasbani has a great eye for things large and small and he knows how to put them together. You leave feeling assured that civilization is not completely in decline. A block south on Yonge, across from the Summerhill LCBO where you can park your car, is the crisply practical kitchenware store **EMBROS**. Good browsing here for fancy imported kitchen stuff, from garlic presses that actually work, to a super-sleek $400 stainless-steel coffee thermos from Germany. Small and delicate **ABSOLUTELY** is mostly about finishing touches for the home (boxes, table lamps, screens, serving pieces). The main inspiration appears to be gently faded classical looks (Empire, Georgian) with a bit of funky '40s and cottage-folk thrown in, just for fun.

Across the street is the uniquely bow-windowed **PRINCE OF SERENDIP** – an apt name, since one usually discovers, serendipitously, the exact thing. The ticket here is outsize and remarkable light fixtures and architectural fragments, which, for their unique scale, often find their way to restaurants or film sets. Across the street, it's a completely different vibe at

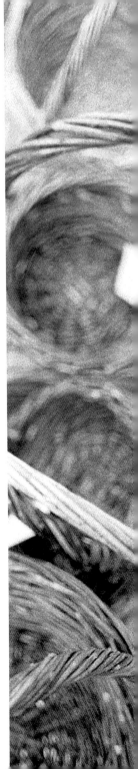

PACK RAT, full of fresh, cottagey looks like rattan furniture uphol-stered in ticking stripes, sisal matting and campaign-style French outdoor furniture.

There are tons of good homey shops in the truly urbane Ave./Dav. corridor. One of my favourites is the idiosyncratic **CONSTANTINE**, with its small yet compelling selection of lamps, throws, pillows and antique furnishings, all with a certain New Age romantic sensibility. Particularly wonderful are the orblike table lamps of coloured Murano glass, the stackable lozenge-shaped velvet buckwheat pillows and Italian throws of rich wool brocade. Antique dealer **STANLEY WAGMAN AND SON**, across the street, is *the* source for fine French antiques, from elegant sculptural deco, to the real thing in rustic French provincial. An excellent place for gilded and glittering chandeliers and sconces, big solid armoires in rich carved woods and the classic bergere.

Also in Yorkville is the Indonesian importer **PRIMITIVES**, which carries new and antique armoires and chaises of beautiful teak. Also eminently desirable are their little teak things, like aged wooden candlesticks and painted intricate temple carvings of coppery green, blue and yellow. And when in Yorkville, check out **ICE**, a truly fab gifty store, filled to the gills with tchatchkes both goofy and divine. From a crocheted strawberry hat for a baby, to a silky tasselled patchwork scarf, they've got it covered. For toys and really silly stuff, I dare you to enter **KIDDING AWOUND** and remain unamused. Their thing is crazy stuff, like a Chinese-made convertible-driving couple that takes your picture ("Photoing on Car") and a stern-faced boxing-nun puppet. Funny cards, too. And, conveniently nearby, under the street level on Cumberland Avenue, is the city's premier stationer, **THE PAPERY**. This store has all the best in bondage materials (ribbon, wrap, boxes, cards and seals) key to great gift presentation.

EN PROVENCE on lovely Hazelton Avenue has exactly what you'd expect: bright, naif Provencal fabrics, traditional French-country furnishings and Med-style tableware, perfect for equipping your own stone *mas*. And don't forget to visit the temple to the body, **ACCA KAPPA**, across the street in the little house that used to house the lovely housewares store, Bleu Nuit. This is the kind of place that makes you want to renounce all your current behaviour and take up a life of ritualistic chanting. A good start would be to take home some of their beautiful natural towels, sponges and brushes, as well as the cleanly packaged body-care line.

Inside the Hazelton Lanes yupscale mini-mall, run directly to **FABRICE**. With absolutely the hottest in costume jewelry, bags, scarves and accessories from Paris, this little place can show you a very good time. More accessory stuff – great belts, hats and hosiery – are also available for dressup play at lower-level **ACCESSITY** on Cumberland Avenue. Perfect for scoring that little *je ne sais quoi* of the season.

To check out **ELTE CARPETS & HOME** megacomplex, you'll have to make a trip out to the Lawrence-Dufferin area, but if you feel like looking at anything from carpets to shower curtains, it will be worth the nosebleed. As the name of the store suggests, Elte's main business is floor coverings (rugs, matts, sisal, broadloom, needlepoint and hardwood flooring), but the concept has expanded to furniture, bedding, bath and home accessories. The look is any way you want it, from wild and ethnic hammered Indian tin to, "we have arrived" (studded leather couches, Italian cotton chenilles and painted ceramic pedestal sinks). Tenants **SUMMERHILL HARDWARE** (a far-flung collection of fittings and knobs) and **GINGER'S** (the latest in taps, sinks, mirrors and soap dishes, like a stainless-steel sink by Philippe Starck that resembles an S&M device) makes this stop a browserama supreme. And, just like at Ikea, there's even somewhere to eat – a groovy little retro-50s diner where you can have lunch or just a cup of coffee.

In the comfortably yuppie Avenue Road and Eglinton area is the pretty **HOMEFRONT**, which stocks beautiful tableware and bed linens with a simple clean, purist look. Watch out for Sophie, the cutest dog in retail who is generally sprawled directly in front of the till. Across the street, tiny **AMELIA'S ORCHARD** is crammed with home furnishings of a more romantic *Out of Africa* bent-tasselled and brocaded pillows and throws in rich coloured damasks and moires.

Another growing *quartier* for home design is centred around the Mount Pleasant and Manor Road area. Here you'll find **HORSE-FEATHERS!** and **FINIALS**. The highly esoteric finds at Horsefeathers' second-floor warehouse (enter from Manor Road) have style. From a 1930s French film cabinet of rubbed stainless steel, to a Russian Byzantine icon headboard, everything's groovy. It's a similar story at neighbouring Finials, a small shop of carefully chosen, vaguely macabre Victoriana – a scary lock of hair preserved in an oval frame, a gilt mirror of small Masonic hands, or a trapezoidal Georgian wine cooler of dark English oak with lions paws.

Across the street is the twiggy headquarters of nouveau gardeners, **HORTICULTURAL DESIGN**, whose design duo keep busy thinking up new and different uses and applications for natural materials like starfish, pinecones, sticks and stones for the home and garden. More gardeny looks, this time of tamer variety, at **SUSAN'S**, an almost completely white shop of touchingly curlicued Victorian painted wicker. For glass and china, drop by **BERNARDI ANTIQUES**. You will feel, of course, like the proverbial bull here (the place is crammed from ceiling to floor with tiny breakable items), but you can find stuff like a corny Aladdin's lamp perfume bottle straight out of "I Dream of Jeannie," or pungently coloured champagne flutes of Murano glass.

If you're in a more robust mood, check out the pricey yet solid selection of folk art collector **SHARON O'DOWD**. She often has strange compelling collectibles like tramp art–framed mirrors and fascinating handmade wooden constructions you'd run off with immediately, if not for the price tag.

DU VERRE: 280 Queen Street West T: 593-0182

URBAN MODE: 389 Queen Street West T: 591-8834

UP COUNTRY: 247 King Street East T: 366-8806

20TH CENTURY: 23 Beverley Street T: 598-2172

QUASIMODO: 789 Queen Street West T: 703-8300

JALAN: 699 Queen Street West T: 504-3473

PAVILION: 670 Queen Street West T: 504-9859; 1915 Queen Street East T: 699-4594

JAPANESE PAPER PLACE: 887 Queen Street West T: 703-0089

MOKUBA: 577 Queen Street West T: 504-5358

TRIANON: 154 King Street East T: 363-9851

L.A. DESIGN: 225 King Street East T: 363-4470

507 ANTIQUES: 50 Carroll Street T: 462-0046

L'ATELIER: 1224 Yonge Street T: 966-0200

EMBROS: 1170 Yonge Street T: 923-1808

ABSOLUTELY: 1132 Yonge Street T: 324-8351

PRINCE OF SERENDIP: 1073 Yonge Street T: 925-3760

PACK RAT: 1062 Yonge Street T: 924-5613

CONSTANTINE: 112 Avenue Road T: 929-1177

STANLEY WAGMAN & SON ANTIQUES: 111 Avenue Road T: 964-1047

PRIMITIVES: 87 Yorkville Avenue T: 967-6357

ICE: 163 Cumberland Street T: 964-6751

KIDDING AWOUND: 91 Cumberland Street T: 926-8996

THE PAPERY: 124 Cumberland Street T: 926-3916

EN PROVENCE: 20 Hazelton Avenue T: 975-9400

ACCA KAPPA: 15 Hazelton Avenue T: 929-5756

FABRICE: 55 Avenue Road T: 967-6590

ACCESSITY: 136 Cumberland Street T: 972-1855

ELTE CARPETS & HOME: 80 Ronald Avenue T: 785-7885

SUMMERHILL DECORATIVE HARDWARE: 80 Ronald Avenue T: 785-1225

GINGER'S BATH CENTRE: 1275 Castlefield Avenue T: 787-1787

HOMEFRONT: 371 Eglinton Avenue West T: 488-3189

AMELIA'S ORCHARD: 394 Eglinton Avenue West T: 486-1057

HORSEFEATHERS!: 630 Mount Pleasant Road T: 486-4555

FINIALS: 705 Mount Pleasant Road T: 481-7588

HORTICULTURAL DESIGN: 608 Mount Pleasant Road T: 488-7716

SUSAN'S ANTIQUES: 585 Mount Pleasant Road T: 487-9262

BERNARDI ANTIQUES: 707 Mount Pleasant Road T: 483-6471

SHARON O'DOWD ANTIQUES: 689 Mount Pleasant Road T: 322-0927

FOOD

Some may flog the virtues of gourmet grocers like **PUSATERI**, **BRUNO'S** or **ZIGGY'S**, or even the various stalls at the somewhat ersatz **ST. LAWRENCE MARKET**, but to my mind, the best place to shop for food in Toronto is **KENSINGTON MARKET**. It's always entertaining and everything in the world is here, from farm-fresh eggs to harissa, and beef empanadas to preserved lemons. The only drawback is the parking crisis on Saturdays. But the parking hassle is worth it for the variety, the prices (half what you pay somewhere fancy) and the market-fresh quality, not to mention the characters you run into along the way.

Baldwin Street, between Spadina and Augusta Avenues is the heart of Kensington and **EUROPEAN MEATS** is ground zero. Take a number at the door and be prepared to get jostled. For the full red-meat experience, grab a hot sausage (knocker, debreceni, bratwurst or Octoberfest) while you wait. There seem to be hundreds of employees wearing orange Super Mario hats and frantically shovelling bundles into numbered plastic bins. Watch out for the big burly types in bloodied lab coats carrying full sides of beef into the store; Saturdays this process is cranked up to fever pitch. My favourite store in

the market for spices and dried fruits and nuts is called, rather literally, **WE SELL AND GRIND ALL KINDS OF COFFEE AND NUTS**. The elegant middle-aged Romanian owner runs this stand as if it were a military base. All the see-through windows of dried fine apricots, figs and pistachios look cared for. Around the corner at 251 Augusta is **THE EGG LADY**. If you've never had same-day eggs, you haven't lived, and this unlabelled storefront sells nothing but ova from the mundane (Grade A large fresh off the truck), to the obscure (giant speckled turkey eggs and tiny quail offspring). And how Kensington can you get? The woman behind the counter, of obviously Eastern European extraction, has been heard speaking fluent Cantonese! And, for more armchair globetrotting, you can snack outside her storefront on either piping-hot empanadas from the Jumbo empanadas stand or crunchy falafels from **ALVAND FOOD MART** right outside her store.

Kensington Avenue, south of Baldwin, is also worth a stroll. One of the highlights is dairy mecca **GLOBAL CHEESE**, deeply amusing for the blaring radio tunes and the jive-talking cheese hustlers behind the counter, mostly obscured behind enormous blocks of cheese. Be sure to come hungry as they practically force-feed you before you buy. Lovely old **SANCI'S** is the spot for tropical fruit. They've been bringing in juicy mangoes and sweet midget honey bananas, as well as dry goods, for their largely Caribbean clientele since 1905 – you can see the date on the old black glass-tile exterior. Unsurprisingly, they always stock the best avocado and fresh thyme, and on a sunny afternoon, they'll be outside sampling perfumey mangoes to passersby. Around the corner on blissfully empty St. Andrew Street is a mini-chicken processing factory called **ST. ANDREW'S POULTRY**. Less store than depot, you dive in behind the counter to procure legs, breasts and thighs from the huge open cases. Jostle for the best pickings. Every winged creature imaginable is represented here in all forms and parts, including feet, necks, giblets and all the requisite stock fixings that Loblaws leaves out.

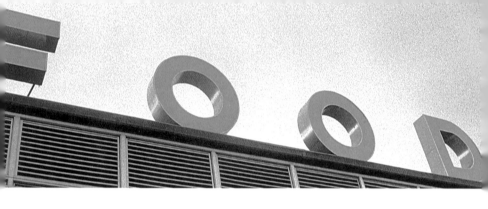

Nearby on Dundas is the old Chinatown (dating back before everybody moved up to Richmond Hill). There are so many great stores in this part of town, you just have to wander and explore (on Sunday this is one of the few areas in Toronto where it's really still rocking), but there are some places you definitely wouldn't want to miss. **FURUYA TRADING COMPANY** is a tiny, tidy Japanese general store. Besides great dry goods (DIY sushi stuff and noodles galore) in fun kitschy food packaging, Furuya carries painted Japanese ceramic plates and bowls, sandals and martial arts outfits. Down the street, you can take a break from the bustle of Chinatown at the hushed and exotic **TEN REN TEA COMPANY**. Important-looking shiny canisters filled with medicinal and curative teas and ginseng line the walls and a geisha-like employee performs a constant tea ceremony in the front window, so you can try before you buy.

One of the city's best historic bakeries, the **HARBORD BAKERY** in the Annex, is still a family favourite. Kids whine for the sweet, eggy braided challah, and the delicious homey cheese danish takes me back to a memorable Budapest clone. Besides the danishes and the rugelach, this bakery's all about bread — they make a mean dark rye, too. Their little gourmet take-out annex, **CALANDRIA**, also makes some of the tastiest take-out food around — sweet, oniony chopped liver (only on weekends), yummy spanokopita, quiches and chicken empanadas. Another Annex-area food-shopping stop is the Hungarian butcher, **ELIZABETH'S DELICATESSEN AND MEAT MARKET**. A warm, paprika-scented baby-blue grocery on Bloor Street West, Elizabeth's is really a gathering place for the Hungarian community, especially on weekends. You can buy things like goose lard and German chocolates, Viennese coffee and traditional dry bacon biscuits, as well as fine sausages, meats and the fruits of the pig, smoked, preserved, in chop or roast form. One block west, you'll find **FORMUSA GOURMET FOODS**, where Joseph Formusa displays his personal collection of olive oils, pastas, dips, vinegars and sauces. For supplies of a healthier variety, check out **NOAH'S NATURAL FOODS**, also on Bloor West. This biggest and best health food store in the city displays organic vegetables and fruits in its window, a macrobiotic mini-café and aisles of vitamins, supplements and potions for body and bath. Try the "living" bread, available in a variety of flavours from the frozen-food section (the carrot-raisin variety is hard to slice but addictive).

Without a doubt, the nerve centre for some of the best fine-food shopping in the city is found at the little strip behind the liquor store at Yonge and Summerhill. Affectionately known as the Five Robbers (for the price tags), these few little stores, in true greengrocer tradition, offer the best of what is available in their own specialty. First stop is **HARVEST WAGON**, where the obscure and perfect fruits and vegetables look so terrific, you could swear they've been flown here first-class (and been given massages and liposuction along the way) from their global points of origin. At any time of year, you can get real tomatoes on the vine from Holland, cute baby vegetables, fresh lemongrass and crisp Fuji apples. The man with the sixth sense about produce is Gus — ask him for the inside scoop. Right behind is **PISCES**, a spit-polished lemon-scented temple to aquatic fare. The Atlantic salmon is particularly delicious (owner George Jung will poach one for you on request), as are the plump sea scallops and littleneck clams. In the middle of the strip, the three storefronts of **ALL THE BEST FINE FOODS** beckon. First comes the prepared-foods chamber, for cheeses (they have an excellent selection of raw sheep's milk and goat cheeses from

France), pricey take-out (muffalettas and spring rolls) and delectable tiny nicoise olives. Next door is the bread department, which is always bustling with people running in to pick up a fresh multigrain before they're all snapped up. Good, cozy, comfy baked goods like giant chunk-chocolate cookies, cranberry upside-down cake and lemon loaf, too. The annexed party supply store always stocks the latest wraps, candles, napkins and greeting cards, all the more convenient for last-minute luxe entertaining. For fleshier matters, go to **OLLIFFE'S**, where the hyper-discriminating butcher, Amos, cracks the whip over his nubile young Rosedale butcher boys. Superb for veal, beef and marinated and prepared dishes like London broil, though steer clear of the overpriced lamb. Great take-out meat sandwiches and greek salad, too.

The Eglinton corridor offers some excellent food shopping as well. The fine butcher, **NICOLA'S**, also sells gourmet-style dry goods, great deli, cheeses and olives and a lovely fresh collection of produce. A great place to stock up when entertaining, or on your way to the cottage, because the store has every food item you might need. If you park across the street, the guy at the booth will give you a ticket that you can have stamped at the cash for free parking. But chiefly, this is the place to buy lamb. Farther west on Eglinton are the best stores for Semitic staples. **NORTOWN** is another butcher's supermarket that's quiet and relaxed until the insanity develops on Fridays, or just before a Jewish high holiday. You shop here for

the unsurpassed barbecue chicken, pink and tender veal chops, oniony latkes and jars of schmaltz (chicken fat, to the uninitiated), for authentic Jewish home cooking. More deli and dry goods down the street at **DAITER'S**, which is especially good for picking up Gryfe's bagels and mini pizzas, Mandel's cream cheese, smoked fish and curious Israeli dry goods like Elite chocolate and Tam-Tam crackers. Across the street is the funny old **HEALTH BREAD BAKERY**, one of the only bakeries in town where you can still buy delicious blueberry buns topped with granules of sugar, dry sweet confections called "nothings" to dip in your tea, and, at Passover, amazing almond macaroons that come stuck on sheets of wax paper. If you're too faded from shopping to cook, drop in to **CHAPMAN'S**, the Forest Hill caterer of choice. This little Eglinton storefront sells prepared food for take-out, as well as the tasty pièce de résistance – tiny festive party sandwiches.

In the northern fringes, there are a couple of notable places to check out. Though Gryfe's bagels are available in more central locations, they still taste better from the source. Tiny **GRYFE'S BAGEL BAKERY** is an aged shop that usually sports a sign saying All Sold Out, unless you happen to luck out and get there early. It seems that they bake a limited number of their heavenly bagels every day, although it has never been made particularly clear why. If there is a Toronto bagel (versus a Montreal bagel), it is Gryfe – chewy on the outside, but fluffy and breadlike in the interior with a salty aftertaste. And it is worth taking a look at **PUSATERI'S** on Avenue Road north of Lawrence. You can't miss it – here's a traffic cop directing the giant lineup of luxury cars vying for a parking space. People don't come here for the produce (it's okay, but not state-of-the-art) or even the excellent meats; they come for the prepared foods and the best of the best in gourmet and exotic condiments and staples. You can purchase every type of oil, vinegar, jam or pasta here, along with fresh-squeezed juices, Godiva chocolate, Kristapson's salmon and Pusateri's own lasagne or home-style scalloped potatoes. It's kind of fun, too – they have the rarified Dean & De Luca New York atmosphere thing down just right. There's always some interesting new gimmick being sampled and lots of bustle and excitement.

An unassuming little bakery that deserves mention is the old-fashioned **LITTLE PIE SHOPPE** on Yonge Street north of Castlefield. Traditionally, it's been where Lawrence Park mothers order their kids' birthday cakes. They have mastered the flower-strewn chocolate slab, as well as baked Canadiana – butter tarts, tea biscuits and hermit cookies, the kind of baked goods we all grew up on before things got so fancy.

Another great shopping neighbourhood to explore is St. Clair West. It's worth exploring virtually every store from Oakwood past Dufferin, but my favourites are, for veggies and fruit as well as Italian dry goods, **ST. CLAIR PRODUCE**, and for meats and cheeses, **CENTRO TRATTORIA FORMAGGI**. St. Clair Produce is the dream grocer with beautiful bushels of peppers, tomatoes, figs or chestnuts, all luscious in season. No Space Age hydroponic airlifted specimens here. This is where families come to buy bushels of tomatoes at the end of the summer, or giant leafy basil plants for their gardens. And you'll find addictive Bistefani biscuits like Alfabotti, Barilla pasta and imported Italian canned tomatoes. More good Barilla-style stuff at Centro Trattoria Formaggi, and delicate prosciutto, the finest grana padano parmesan, fresh bocconcini and tangy dried black olives. And while you shop, you can go for a little something in their little rear tavola calda, say, chicken with mushrooms or the delicious ricotta-filled canneloni.

By now, almost everyone knows the city's best smoked salmon comes from **KRISTAPSON'S**. It's so mouth-watering, you had best call to order a belly before driving all that way east on Queen; they're often sold out in advance on holidays. Nothing else for sale here except jars of honey – puzzling.

Another important food-shopping destination is Little Portugal at the edge of College West. For satisfying little flans with black caramelized tops and toothsome heavy cornbread, visit the **NOVA ESTORIL BAKERY**, open seven days a week. Virtually next door is **CHURRASQUEIRA DOWNTOWN**. Go there for churrasco-style barbecued chicken, so juicy it runs down your chin. Nearby on Ossington south of College is another great fish store – this one in a charmingly old aluminum exterior. **PEIXARIA PORTUGAL** is spanking clean and odourless inside, the fish fresh and glossy on constantly replenished beds of crushed ice.

EUROPEAN MEATS: 176 Baldwin Street T: 596-8691

THE EGG LADY: 251 Augusta Avenue T: unlisted

GLOBAL CHEESE SHOP: 76 Kensington Avenue T: 593-9251

WE SELL AND GRIND ALL KINDS OF COFFEE AND NUTS: 202 Baldwin Street T: unlisted

SANCI'S TROPICAL FOODS: 66 Kensington Avenue T: 593-9265

ST. ANDREW POULTRY: 17 St. Andrew Street T: 596-7305

FURUYA TRADING COMPANY: 460 Dundas Street West T: 977-5451

TEN REN TEA COMPANY: 454 Dundas Street West T: 598-7872

HARBORD BAKERY & CALANDRIA: 115 Harbord Street T: 922-5767

ELIZABETH'S DELICATESSEN AND MEAT MARKET: 410 Bloor Street West T: 921-8644

FORMUSA GOURMET FOODS: 480 Bloor Street West T: 537-8563

NOAH'S NATURAL FOODS: 322 Bloor Street West T: 968-7930

VIENNA HOME BAKERY: 626 Queen Street West T: 703-7278

HARVEST WAGON: 1103 Yonge Street T: 923-7542

OLLIFFE'S: 1097 Yonge Street T: 928-0296

PISCES: 1103 Yonge Street T: 921-8888

ALL THE BEST FINE FOODS: 1099 Yonge Street T: 928-3330

NICOLA'S CHOICE MEATS: 298 Eglinton Avenue West T: 485-4429

NORTOWN FOODS LIMITED: 892 Eglinton Avenue West T: 789-2921

DAITER'S CREAMERY AND APPETIZERS: 928 Eglinton Avenue West T: 787-5913

HEALTH BREAD BAKERY: 947 Eglinton Avenue West T: 782-2891

CHAPMAN'S FINE FOODS: 1114 Eglinton Avenue West T: 636-9009

GRYFE'S BAGEL BAKERY: 3421 Bathurst Street T: 783-1552

PUSATERI'S: 1539 Avenue Road T: 785-9100

THE LITTLE PIE SHOPPE: 2568 Yonge Street T: 485-6393

ST. CLAIR PRODUCE: 1036 St. Clair Avenue West T: 654-4600

CENTRO TRATTORIA FORMAGGI: 1224 St. Clair Avenue West T: 656-8111

KRISTAPSON'S: 1095 Queen Street East T: 466-5152

NOVA ESTORIL BAKERY: 673 College Street T: 532-6093

CHURRASQUEIRA DOWNTOWN: 671 College Street T: not available

PEIXARIA PORTUGAL: 222 Ossington Avenue T: 537-6276

SHOPPING ADVENTURES

Excellent adventures in shopping happen when you stumble across a place that has an air of undiscovered mystery. One of the most fun places to shop is the wildly idiosyncratic budget department store, **HONEST ED'S**. Three floors of below-retail madness spread between two buildings at the corner of Bloor and Bathurst Streets with its own quirky set of rules. First, the store doesn't open until noon, and all morning, under the Vegas-style sign ("Don't just stand there, buy something!"), an assortment of budget hounds, retirees and street people who are convinced they're being controlled by aliens, populate the lineup for Ed's door-crasher specials. Once inside, you're surrounded by picked-over aisles of stuff, bombarded by interrogation-quality lighting and the loudly projected voice of the otherworldly in-store announcer, and loving it. Typically, the best finds are in the kitchen and housewares department, where you get great value on items like Italian ceramic pasta bowls with pretty painted rims, saintly votive candles, nonstick cookware and restaurant supply.

The below-ground food level is fab for unusual foodstuffs from around the world, like German coffee, Israeli dry soup, Swiss chocolate and West Indian condiments. On the same floor is the hardware department, which is nuts just before Christmas, with absolutely the wildest in tree decorations and home decor. On the main floor, the pharmacy area, notoriously cheap, has humorously packaged hair-care and skin preparations. There are always surprises in the toy department, as well, like a cheap cooking set or knockoff Barbie doll from Red China. On the upper levels are clothes (infant layettes and men's stuff is the best bet), as well as towels and linens in sombre cottons from former East Bloc countries. While exploring the store is always fun, the headache begins at the checkout, which is still, somewhat charmingly in this day and age, completely unautomated. This means that you have to wait, lugging your giant plastic sacks of booty through the seemingly endless lines.

For shopping fun of the fashion variety, try **TOM'S PLACE** in Kensington Market. Located between a fish purveyor and a dried-fruit store on Baldwin, this designer discount store for men and women is run by the dashing Tom Mihalik and his family. Many of the items have cut-out designer labels, so you'll have to rely on your refined fashion sense for guidance. It's up to you to determine whether that ruffled polka-dot silk is indeed a Valentino, or the long black morning jacket a Suzie Tompkins. These details are all germane when it comes both to successfully picking through the racks and negotiating prices on the way out. You see, as in the Budapest market, none of these fabulous threads comes with a price tag – you have to haggle with Tom at the cash, and he's good.

Nearby on Spadina is the giant Asian kitchenware source, **TAP PHONG TRADING**. Stroll through the aisles of stuff: compelling red and gold Chinese party supplies, banquet hall–size stockpots, affordable wicker tea caddies, brightly coloured kids' chopsticks and every kind of glass cup and bowl imaginable is available at great prices. Also, Tap Phong never seems to close, so you can avail yourself of its pleasures whenever the spirit moves you. Another restaurant supply that's fun to explore, though much smaller, is hip **NIKOLAOU** on Queen West near Spadina. The best in juicers, graters, whisks and other kitchen necessaries, as well as colourful stuff like the full rainbow of Fiesta ware. The guys who run it are kind of cute and flirty, too.

For funky toys, there are tons of wholesalers on Spadina that will happily let you explore. One of the best is **SUPERIOR WHOLESALER**, for beautiful, retro-looking, all-metal model cars, planes, helicopters, the lot imported from China. You know, the kind that they don't make here anymore because they're potentially dangerous. There are also large bins of cheapie party favours for kids' birthdays, say, a case of plastic animals (jungle, farm or dinosaur). Another classic novelty store is **ONTARIO SPECIALTY COMPANY** on Church Street. All the great toys: real made-in-China five-and-dime stuff, plastic food and collector's pieces, like the battery-powered knight in armour, fully prepared for a jousting match on horseback. But don't think for a minute that you can get the owners to crack a smile at your antics with the miniatures – they've seen it all before.

There is, however, one novelty store where they really get the joke. **FUN-O-RAMA** on Queen Street West is a wild gallery of novelties, some valuable and vintage, and some just terrifically amusing crap like the

Happy Days board game or Bionic Man collectible action figures. The place looks like some geeky guy's bedroom, complete with little mystery drawers of more arcane collections, like hundreds of plastic eyeballs or teensy toothbrushes. And the creator and proprietor of this amusement-park-in-miniature is Morris Greenbaum, who's always happy to further amuse you with tales of his collecting adventures.

For dress-up, go adventuring at **MALABAR'S** on McCaul Street. This is the place where the dance, opera and ballet companies rent their costumes, and you can, too. Be Marie Antoinette for a day, or night. Halloween is a great time to shop here, of course – they have every wig and makeup effect imaginable inside their giant old smelly rad building. And hanging around the cash is a large and egocentric feline named Jack, a big black male who considers himself the star of the whole event.

Say you want to create something for your home or closet with wild and wonderful fabrics. Your best bet is to schlep out to **DESIGNER FABRIC OUTLET** in Parkdale. If you drive all the way there, find a parking space and make it past *les misérables* on the sidewalk, you're halfway there. D.F.O. stocks every textile imaginable, from plain cotton ticking on canvas, to exquisite Belgian chenilles and brilliant Thai silk. Much of what they sell are ends of bolts, so there are lots of surprises, and you can find some very good fabrics. The downside is that you won't find any more of it, so come armed with knowledge – pillow sizes or how much material you need for your special project. If you're unsure about your purchase, samples of all the bolts are displayed near the cash in the front and you can borrow them to try at home. Check out their trim annex, an entire room of trim, from rickrack to tassels, pillow forms and drapery necessities, to inspire your creativity. For the bright and beautiful traditional African raiment, Kente cloth, try **MANASSEH** on Bathurst Street, north of Bloor. In this small shop full of regal black women wearing magnificent headpieces, you can buy these fabrics by the yard along with truly fabulous ready-to-wear and custom clothing. And if you're really nice, the owner may give you some of her authentic shea butter to take home. Same story, different beat at beautiful, exotic **MAHARANI FASHIONS**, on Gerrard Street in Little India. Intricate sari fabrics of embroidered and metallic silks (which can double as impromptu tablecloths, curtains, throws or runners) line the walls, plus racks of extravagant evening getups and shimmering accessories. A cheap thrill are the handwoven silk organza shawls in green, blue, orange, red and rainbow hues, for only fifteen bucks.

If you're without a giant trust fund, you probably don't do all your Christmas shopping at **CHANEL** or **HERMES**. However, it is great juicy fun to explore these super-luxe palaces of desire, just to fondle really gorgeous things, like full-length red suede gloves or divine blue-and-black Hermes blankets and then giggle at the price tags. Just so you don't immediately run out depressed by the attitude visited upon you by the sales staff, here's a tip: don't enter these hallowed halls in your study clothes. Even browsing here requires lipstick and lots of swagger. Best to make an entrance after a long, boozy Yorkville lunch.

Sam Mirshak, the relaxed and gentle owner of **THE DOOR STORE** on Britain Street behind the Queen East auction houses, has amassed a collection of architectural fragments and iron pieces from France, marble mantels and new and antique doorknobs and pulls of every vintage and variety. This is really a design source, a place to come and be inspired by beautiful materials where you can think and create in peace. It's a similar story at the offbeat **STEPTOE & WIFE**. This small Davenport metal fabricator imports exotic materials like Victorian enamelled tiles, embossed anaglypta wall coverings, mouldings and decorative enrichments from around the world. Should you fail to find something that twigs your fancy, you can order it at either of these places – they will show you books of materials from suppliers, both famed and obscure.

For art treasures, there are great discoveries at **D & E LAKE** on King East. You'll find a wonderful collection of antique books on art, design and architecture, as well as bins of vintage etchings, engravings and prints, organized by subject matter and artist. You'll also discover old maps, amusing watercolours or pretty botanicals, and in the backroom, you have your choice of frames. For more contemporary but still affordable work, it's worth visiting the second-floor atelier of **ART INTERIORS** on Spadina Road, where clever young proprietresses Lisa Diamond and Shira Wood display the wares of up-and-coming painters and printmakers. You can get anything here, from a large-scale oil landscape, to a tiny, witty print, and they'll frame it for you, too.

My favourite auction house is **RITCHIE'S** on King East. What's great about it is the somewhat down-at-heels glamour. At previews, which are advertised in the newspaper, you'll see everything from a Morris side chair, to super-funky Suzie Cooper dishes from the '40s, to a magnificent Aubusson that shows its age. This stuff is not overly refinished or gleaming with polish, but rather elegantly worn, and so prices tend to be affordable. Exploring here is relaxed and employees are virtually attitude-free.

One of the best shopping adventures doesn't even involve a store. **FRANK J. CORRENTI CIGARS** is a tiny manufacturer of hand-rolled Cuban cigars on the second floor of a dilapidated garment-district building. Inside, a handful of middle-aged women roll stogies while

casually puffing away on a fat one. Everybody smokes here – the walls are glazed a nicotine yellow that faux painters would envy. The tobacco is imported in sheets from Cuba and hand-rolled into fat Churchills or suave Monte Cristo's and sold to dealers throughout the city. You can buy your own here; if you buy bulk, Correnti's will even affix your own label to them before shoving them into those round metal canisters that are used for ice cream in Asia.

HONEST ED'S: 581 Bloor Street West **T:** 537-1574

TOM'S PLACE: 190 Baldwin Street **T:** 596-0297

TAP PHONG TRADING: 360 Spadina Avenue **T:** 977-6364

NIKOLAOU: 629 Queen Street West **T:** 504-6411

SUPERIOR WHOLESALER: 422 Spadina Avenue **T:** 593-9890

ONTARIO SPECIALTY COMPANY: 133 Church Street **T:** 366-9327

FUN-O-RAMA: 618 Queen Street West **T:** 504-0945

MALABAR'S: 14 McCaul Street **T:** 598-2581

DESIGNER FABRIC OUTLET: 1360 Queen Street West **T:** 531-2810

MANASSEH: 996 Bathurst Street **T:** 535-7447

MAHARANI FASHIONS: 1417 Gerrard Street East **T:** 466-8400

CHANEL BOUTIQUE: 131 Bloor Street West **T:** 925-2577

HERMES: 131 Bloor Street West **T:** 968-8626

THE DOOR STORE: 43 Britain Street **T:** 863-1590

STEPTOE & WIFE ANTIQUES LIMITED: 322 Geary Avenue **T:** 530-4200

D & E LAKE LIMITED: 237 King Street **T:** East 863-9930

ART INTERIORS: 446 Spadina Road **T:** 208 488-3157

RITCHIE'S: 288 King Street East **T:** 364-1864

FRANK J. CORRENTI CIGARS: 443 King Street West **T:** 596-6597

activities

COOL MUSEUMS & GALLERIES

Even though there's very little in the way of world-class art in this our world-class city (unless you feel a mystic connection to the works of Henry Moore), there are some goodies at the big museums and galleries.

Now that the **ART GALLERY OF ONTARIO** (AGO) has been tucked, rouged and lifted, it's an even prettier place to hang out. The Walker Court was always lovely with its frieze of Indian tribal names in Greco-Roman lettering, but now there's way more to enjoy: the magnificent Etruscan red rooms of recent European paintings grandly framed and mounted floor to ceiling; the totally fun hands-on playroom for kids; the glass-walled Tanenbaum Gallery school; and some minor Fauvist works right after you walk in on the main floor. There's also a beautiful Patterson Ewen weather triptych as you enter the gallery. The best way to visit the AGO is as a member; not only do you get free admission each time you come, you can pause for a drink or a cup of coffee in the charming members' lounge on the second floor, an ideal place to hide on a rainy afternoon.

For state-of-the-art weird, check out the always-chic shows at the **S. L. SIMPSON** in the former Original Furniture Company on Queen Street West. General Idea used to show here when they were still up and kicking, and that's the kind of stuff you see at the Simpson – political, challenging and somewhat puzzling. Same story at the **POWER PLANT** at Harbourfront, a beautiful, open, former industrial space on the water, with ever-changing exhibits that

never upstage the grandeur of the bright open space. Warning: the experience often involves intricate, virtually incomprehensible, manifesto statements.

THE DESIGN EXCHANGE on Wellington Street is worth a look if only for the beautiful '30s building, the former Stock Exchange – the magnificent period trading hall has been preserved. The Exchange is all about excellence in interdisciplinary design (furniture, product and fashion design) with a design bookstore, **INDX**, on the main floor. If you're in the neighbourhood but feel a little less highbrow, do the Canuck thing and visit the **HOCKEY HALL OF FAME** in the BCE Place. Maybe you'll meet some really hunky hockey buffs; just don't snicker during the moments of silence before player shrines.

THE ROYAL ONTARIO MUSEUM, the ROM to familiars, has excellent dinosaur exhibits for kids, with just the right blend of fright-inducing thrill and interactive button-pushing. Largely unchanged since the early '70s, the displays are still good, especially the diorama of the archaeologist wrapping bones in plaster that for some reason holds endless fascination for the under twelves. More thrills and chills in the Batcave, a *son et lumière* show of spooky strobelights and fluttering bat-wing sounds. And don't miss: the bird room, with its many drawers of eggs and bird droppings; the calming dappled boreal forest and marsh-land dioramas; the great Chinese stuff on the main floor; and the dusty mummies.

The **BATA SHOE MUSEUM**, in its grand new Raymond Moriyama–designed home at St. George and Bloor, houses the massive personal collection of shoe czarina Sonya Bata. It never fails to amaze, either torturous primitive footwear, or Elton John's glitterock platform boots should fascinate. Another highly specialized collection, though less well known, is the **MUSEUM FOR TEXTILES** on Centre Street. With rotating exhibits, like the best of needlework guru Kaffe Fassett, as well as a permanent collection of fine textiles (African mudcloths and Asian indigo–dyed and woodblock-patterned prints), it's actually quite groovy. I also really like the small, specialized **GEORGE R. GARDINER MUSEUM OF CERAMIC ART**, across the street from the ROM. Its thing is porcelain, from Meissen to Majolica, and it also features a fine collection of painted porcelain commedia dell'arte figures hidden away on the second floor that is really worth a look. Visit at Christmastime, when the museum puts on a show of twelve trees by local designers.

For photography, the place to go is the **JANE CORKIN GALLERY** on John Street. Corkin trades in the finest photographs on the world market and shows all the biggies (Man Ray, Brassai, Eisenstaedt), as well as more unconventional, less well known photographers. But since there's very little in the way of wall space here, you may find yourself perusing the open bins of photographs on file for the more interesting finds. If you feel like gallery hopping, move from here to the **MERCER UNION** on King West, where something fascinating yet cryptic, like piled-up garbage in the shape of Newfoundland, is always happening, or walk south on Spadina to 80 Spadina Avenue. With the entire building devoted to small galleries, it's perfect for gallery hopping indoors on a nasty day. (Don't miss the **ALBERT WHITE**

and **LEO KAMEN** galleries, they're almost always worthwhile.)

One little-known gallery worth a visit is **ARTIA**, Vladimir Purghart's soul-stirring collection of museum-quality Russian fine arts. The magnificent, often wildly coloured icons and Soviet realist artifacts are often bizarre, yet fascinating, and the characteristically impassioned Vladimir uses his great knowledge and impressive physical presence to almost hypnotic effect. Not an everyday experience. Less intense is **ED'S THEATRE MUSEUM** open weekend afternoons only, on top of Old Ed's, in the Ed's Warehouse restaurant complex. The completely bizarre collection of costumes, props and sets collected by none other than Sir Mirvish himself is vastly entertaining, especially after a martini and roast beef lunch.

Art queen **YDESSA HENDELES** has a private gallery on King Street that is a surreal experience. In an old uniform factory (the cool signage remains), she has created a highly personal salon. None of the work is for sale; seems she just does this to aid in the education of the masses. The other local art diva, **OLGA KORPER**, is less altruistic. Like Hendeles, she also renovated an industrial edifice to house her gallery. But she will sell you the pubic-hair sculpture by her dining-room table.

ART GALLERY OF ONTARIO: 317 Dundas Street West T: 977-0414

S. L. SIMPSON GALLERY: 515 Queen Street West T: 504-3738

POWER PLANT: Harbourfront Centre, Queen's Quay West T: 973-4949

THE DESIGN EXCHANGE: 234 Bay Street T: 363-6121

ROYAL ONTARIO MUSEUM: 100 Queen's Park Crescent T: 586-5549

HOCKEY HALL OF FAME: 30 Yonge Street T: 360-7735

BATA SHOE MUSEUM: 327 Bloor Street West T: 979-7799

MUSEUM FOR TEXTILES: 55 Centre Avenue T: 599-5321

GEORGE R. GARDINER MUSEUM OF CERAMIC ART: 111 Queen's Park T: 586-8080

THE JANE CORKIN GALLERY: 179 John Street T: 979-1980

MERCER UNION: 439 King Street West T: 977-1412

ALBERT WHITE GALLERY: 80 Spadina Avenue T: 703-1021

LEO KAMEN GALLERY: 80 Spadina Avenue T: 504-9515

ARTIA: 620 Richmond Street West T: 865-1255

ED'S THEATRE MUSEUM: 276 King Street West T: 974-9378

YDESSA HENDELES ART FOUNDATION: 778 King Street West T: 413-9400

OLGA KORPER GALLERY: 17 Morrow Avenue T: 538-8220

THEATRES & CINEMAS

Toronto is a major centre for live theatre, but it's often hard to get it together to go. First, you usually have to buy tickets in advance. Then, you actually have to be at the theatre on time for the eight o'clock curtain or they won't let you in. This is a serious drawback for those who are terminally late, or can't commit to any kind of plan-making. Worst of all, if you do get to the theatre on time, the performance can be horrible, and a play is way harder to walk out on than a bad movie.

The big theatres all possess their special charms. The most endearing is Ed Mirvish's **ROYAL ALEXANDRA THEATRE**, with its retro flocked-velvet wall coverings and heavy baroque theatricality. At intermission, there's a good, slightly seedy scene around the bar, where the throngs lining up for drink tickets are soothed by the odd musical strains of the visiting piano stylist. The shows are dicey, usually light musicals or comedies that grate on the nerves, so a subscription is out of the question. However, if something good is in town with a terrific lead (say, Alan Bates in Ibsen's *The Master Builder*), run and grab a ticket. The best seats are generally in the front row of the first balcony; avoid the second balcony for vertical potential. More glittering, less soulful perhaps is the newly constructed Mirvish venue, **PRINCESS OF WALES THEATRE**. Designed by Yabu Pushelberg and purpose-built for the mega production *Les Misérables*, it's worth the visit for the washrooms alone. Also lovely are the rejuvenated **ELGIN** and **WINTER GARDEN THEATRES**. The larger Elgin Theatre on the lower level is comparatively sombre but for its domed ceiling (just right for Opera Atelier's Mozart productions). The real treat is the smaller upstairs Winter Garden which retains its 1913 illusion of a misty clearing in the woods, with real leaves and lanterns covering the ceiling. If you've never had a chance to attend a performance here, you must take the opportunity. Also pretty is the **PANTAGES THEATRE**, which was completely rebuilt to house the blockbuster *Phantom of the Opera*. However, its current grandeur seems a bit nouveau, considering it was originally opened in 1920 for vaudeville and silent films, the people's entertainment of the era. Around the corner is lovely old MASSEY HALL, where Gordon Lightfoot books in for a week every year. Performers love this venue for its amazing acoustics and intimate aura, but audiences dislike the seats with obstructed views.

Everyone makes fun of the O'KEEFE CEN-TRE – soon to be renamed the HUMMING-BIRD CENTRE – which is the home of the ballet and Canadian Opera Company, for now. But there is a certain charm to the goofy '60s building, even with its terrible acoustics. Everything plays here, from tribal Japanese drummers to Tom Jones and, if there's ever a show where you really want to rock, this is a great place because there's lots of room to dance in the aisles. I once saw Gladys Knight and the Pips here – the totally Motown crowd got down in a major way. Plus, they sell delicious Callard & Bowser toffees in the lobby. People also mock ROY THOMSON HALL'S nuclear plant exterior, but the Arthur Erickson–designed concert hall glitters inside. You can watch the symphony play, or listen to renowned

international performers of classical music and jazz in the Great Performers' series. Despite its large size (seats almost 3,000), there is an extraordinary feeling of intimacy. The urban myth is that none of the seats is more than 100 feet away from the stage, though that seems hard to believe. So, it's a great place to come and hear Pinchas Zukerman, but a terrible place for a benefit or a premiere. At the party in the lobby, the endless rotunda becomes annoying – you spend the entire evening searching for the rest of your group.

For dance other than ballet, venture down to the somewhat desolate Queen's Quay Terminal, where on the upper level, you will find the **PREMIERE DANCE THEATRE**. Specifically built for dance performance, it achieves a neat, intimate, though rather colourless setting for observing whirling figures from international dance companies as well as our own local lights: Danny Grossman, Desrosiers and the Toronto Dance Theatre.

Generally, you can trust the productions at only a few of the smaller theatres. Judge by the playwrights and actors instead of the space. The **TARRAGON THEATRE** on Bridgeman Avenue is always good for budding works of genius by terrific Canadian playwrights such as Michael Tremblay and Judith Thompson, and there's an excellent group of actors that frequent the theatre's two stages (Clare Coulter, R. H. Thomson, et al). The venue affords a cozy sort of off-Broadway experience, with the larger space downstairs hosting the major productions and the Extra Space upstairs used for more experimental works. The theatre community goes Sundays, because those are PWYC (pay what you can) shows. Other hip theatres worth checking out are the **FACTORY THEATRE** on Bathurst Street which also showcases new Canadian plays, and **THEATRE PASSE MURAILLE** on Ryerson Avenue with its large Mainspace for mainstream productions and tiny Backspace for the really way-out. If you hear or read about any plays involving Leah

Cherniak, Daniel Brooks, Richard Rose or Theatre Smith Gilmour, go; it should be an interesting night.

The best first-run movie theatres, for atmosphere, sound and screen pyrotechnics are the classy Pink Panther–era **YORK**, deco jewel the **EGLINTON** and the nasty old **UPTOWN**. The upstairs theatre at the York is the most felicitous venue for a film you really want to see and hear. It boasts a giant screen, T.H.X. sound that will blow you out of your chair and lots of seats, so you won't get shut out of even the most popular flick. The pretty Eglinton is a period gem with a junior lobby but a wonderful old-Hollywood feel, with its deco figureheads and balcony. Good picture quality and rip-roaring sound are excellent for epic-type adventure pics. You go to the Uptown to see an action movie, preferably one with multiple explosions in the large screen behind the candy bar on the second floor. Sit in the balcony, 'cause it shakes.

The best art films and foreign flicks end up at the **CARLTON**, which is unfortunately a miniplex of airless screening closets. If you're lucky, the same film might be playing at the independent **REGENT** on Mount Pleasant, an old-style theatre where the proprietor actually greets you

Saturday evenings in a tux. Sometimes, art films also end up at the Famous Players showcase theatre, the **CUMBERLAND FOUR**, totally scary for its stuffed-apple dolls in the lobby and "golden topping" on the popcorn, not to mention its odd multiple levels. Possibly the worst place to see a first-run film is the horrible **PLAZA THEATRE** under the Hudson's Bay Centre at Yonge and Bloor, where you take an escalator underground that rivals the ancient endless escalators in the London tube. Comfortable cinema chairs, though. The **PLAZA** escalator trip is seconded only by the creepy **MARKET SQUARE CINEPLEX**, which is almost always virtually empty (a bonus when a film's just opened) and involves the same hair-raising ride into the bowels of the theatre.

The only true art theatre left in town with any integrity is the freezing old **REVUE** on Roncesvalles Avenue. Even though it's owned by Festival Cinemas, the consortium that owns the **BLOOR**, **FOX** and **KINGSWAY** theatres, it seems to play films that aren't just second-run Hollywood but actually a bit more interesting. Same story at the extremely west **PARADISE**, which persists in showing decent films like *Wings of Desire* or *Raging Bull* despite the fact that the theatre will be almost empty. Reg Hartt's **CINEFORUM** on Bathurst is always different; its specialty is the charmingly titled Sex and Violence Cartoon Festival, and odd bits like an uncut print of the 1934 Nuremberg rally.

For a giant epic film, go to the **CINESPHERE** at Ontario Place. The height of Imax wizardry when it was built, it still manages to blow me away with the sheer magnitude of the picture and force of the sound. Warning: Going stoned, and sitting in the middle rows of the Cinesphere's wraparound screen to see *Apocalypse Now* is not for the faint-of-heart.

THEATRES

ROYAL ALEXANDRA THEATRE: 260 King Street West Tickets: 872-1212; 1-800-461-3333

PRINCESS OF WALES THEATRE: 300 King Street West T: 872-1212

ELGIN AND WINTER GARDEN THEATRES: 189-191 Yonge Street T: 363-5353

PANTAGES THEATRE: 244 Victoria Street T: 872-2222

MASSEY HALL: 178 Victoria Street T: 363-7301

HUMMINGBIRD CENTRE: (formerly O'Keefe Centre) 1 Front Street East T: 393-7469

TARRAGON THEATRE: 30 Bridgeman Avenue T: 536-5018

FACTORY THEATRE: 125 Bathurst Street T: 504-9971

THEATRE PASSE MURAILLE: 16 Ryerson Avenue T: 504-7529

PREMIERE DANCE THEATRE: Queen's Quay Terminal Building, Queen's Quay West
T: 973-4000

ROY THOMSON HALL: 60 Simcoe Street Tickets: 872-4255

CINEMAS

YORK: 101 Eglinton Avenue East T: 486-5600

EGLINTON: 400 Eglinton Avenue West T: 487-4721

UPTOWN: 764 Yonge Street T: 922-3113

CARLTON: 20 Carlton Street T: 598-2309

REGENT: 551 Mount Pleasant Road T: 480-9884

CUMBERLAND FOUR: 159 Cumberland Street T: 964-5970

PLAZA THEATRE: Hudson's Bay Centre, Yonge and Bloor T: 964-2555

MARKET SQUARE CINEPLEX: 80 Front Street East T: 364-2300

REVUE: 400 Roncesvalles Avenue T: 531-9959

BLOOR: 506 Bloor Street West T: 532-6677

FOX: 2236 Queen Street East T: 691-7330

KINGSWAY: 3030 Bloor Street West T: 236-1411

PARADISE: 1006 Bloor Street West T: 537-7040

CINEFORUM: 463 Bathurst Street T: 603-3022

CINESPHERE: Ontario Place, 955 Lakeshore Boulevard West T: 314-9900

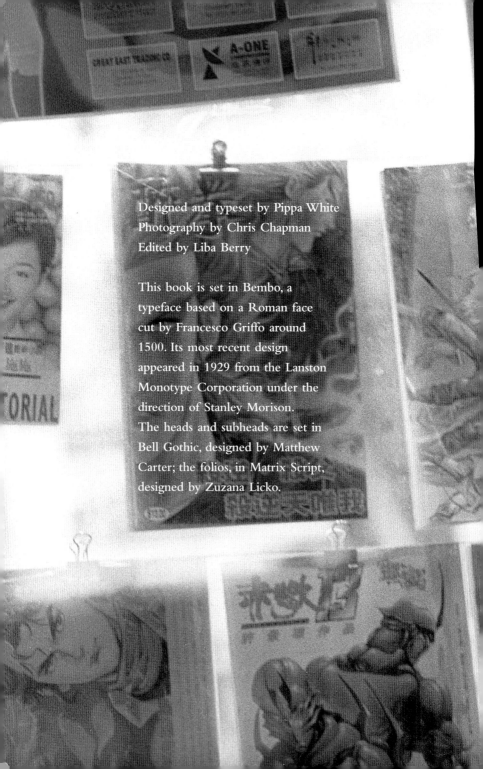

Designed and typeset by Pippa White
Photography by Chris Chapman
Edited by Liba Berry

This book is set in Bembo, a
typeface based on a Roman face
cut by Francesco Griffo around
1500. Its most recent design
appeared in 1929 from the Lanston
Monotype Corporation under the
direction of Stanley Morison.
The heads and subheads are set in
Bell Gothic, designed by Matthew
Carter; the folios, in Matrix Script,
designed by Zuzana Licko.